PRAISE FOR

SEVEN DAYS THAT DIVIDE THE WORLD

This book is a delight to read. It is thoughtful, perceptive, friendly, and bold when it needs to be. Dr. Lennox has gone right to the heart of the matter in his thinking about Genesis and the age of the earth, and how that is a different question from purposeless evolution. In this well-written book, which shows good learning accessibly presented, Dr. Lennox has helped us think clearly about these questions. I look forward to sharing this book with many people. Thank you, Dr. Lennox!

C. John Collins, professor of Old Testament,
Covenant Theological Seminary

This remarkable book by John Lennox is exactly what I've been looking to recommend! Its treatment of Genesis 1 and 2 in connection with modern science and ancient Near Eastern culture is accessible, wide-ranging, balanced, and irenic. Lennox has written a wise, well-informed work, and it deserves the widest readership possible.

Paul Copan, professor and Pledger Family chair
of philosophy and ethics, Palm Beach Atlantic
University, West Palm Beach, Florida

Dr. Lennox is an apt guide for exploring both the Bible and science. He admirably argues that they both reveal the same Creator and Designer. In this careful and well-documented study, he examines all the pertinent issues concerning the meaning of the Genesis creation account. Every careful reader will come away more knowledgeable, wiser, and better able to defend the truth of the Bible before a skeptical world.

Doug Groothuis, professor of philosophy, Denver Seminary, and author of *Christian Apologetics*

Seven Days That Divide the World will certainly be controversial, but it is worthy of a careful reading by those interested in the ongoing science/religion discussion.

Dr. Henry F. Schaefer III, Graham Perdue professor of chemistry and director of the Center for Computational Quantum Chemistry, University of Georgia

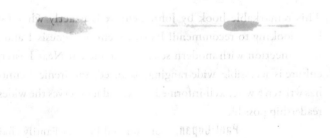

SEVEN DAYS

THAT DIVIDE THE WORLD

10TH ANNIVERSARY EDITION

SEVEN DAYS

DAYS

THAT DIVIDE THE WORLD

THE BEGINNING ACCORDING TO
GENESIS AND **SCIENCE**

10th Anniversary Edition

JOHN C. LENNOX

**ZONDERVAN
REFLECTIVE**

ZONDERVAN REFLECTIVE

Seven Days That Divide the World, 10th Anniversary Edition
Copyright © 2011, 2021 by John C. Lennox

Requests for information should be addressed to:
Zondervan, *3900 Sparks Dr. SE, Grand Rapids, Michigan 49546*

Zondervan titles may be purchased in bulk for educational, business, fundraising, or sales promotional use. For information, please email SpecialMarkets@Zondervan.com.

ISBN 978-0-310-12781-9 (softcover)
ISBN 978-0-310-12783-3 (audio)
ISBN 978-0-310-12782-6 (ebook)

Cover design: Thinkpen Design
Cover photo: Silas Baisch / Unsplash
Interior design: Sara Colley

Printed in the United States of America

HB 04.04.2024

For Larry Taunton –
whose idea it was

CONTENTS

Appendices

PREFACE TO THE SECOND EDITION

Ten years have passed since the first edition of this book. During those years I have been gratified to hear from many people who have been kind enough to say that they found its content helpful in enabling them to see that the major controversy with which it engages can be resolved without compromising commitment to the authority of Scripture. I am also grateful to those people who have sent me their criticisms and comments. In light of them it became clear the book needed revision, both to avoid misunderstandings and to make corrections. I am grateful to Dr. Paul Marston for his helpful input, particularly from his perspective as a historian of science, and to Stephen Shaw QC for running his legal eye past my arguments and enabling me to tighten them up. In launching this new edition it is my hope that it will provide food for thought for a new generation of readers.

John Lennox, Oxford, June 2020

ACKNOWLEDGEMENTS

I have benefitted over the years from interactions with many people and from reading many books and commentaries, but I am chiefly indebted to my lifelong friend and mentor the late Professor David Gooding, Member of the Royal Irish Academy. It was he who first drew my attention many years ago to the fact that Genesis 1 is concerned not simply with creation, but also with organization. I also owe to him innumerable insights into the riches of the Bible that have influenced me so profoundly that they have become an intrinsic part of my thinking. I would like to thank Barbara Hamilton for her invaluable help in spotting grammatical and stylistic infelicities in my original manuscript. I am also indebted to my research assistant, Simon Wenham, for his constant, cheerful input and critical eye.

INTRODUCTION

BEGINNING AT THE BEGINNING

"In the beginning, God created the heavens and the earth." These majestic words introduce the most translated, most printed, and most read book in history. I well remember how profoundly they affected me on Christmas Eve 1968, when as a student at Cambridge University I heard them read to the watching world on live television by the crew of Apollo 8 as they orbited the moon. The context was a triumphant achievement of science and technology that caught the imagination of the millions of people who watched it. To celebrate that success the astronauts chose to read a text that needed no added explanation or qualification, even though it was written millennia ago. The biblical announcement of the fact of creation was as timelessly clear as it was magnificently appropriate.

However, as distinct from the fact of creation, when it

comes to the *timing* and *means* of creation, particularly the interpretation of the famous sequence of days with which the book begins, people over the centuries have found the book of Genesis less easy to understand. Indeed, controversy about this matter is at an all-time high, with the debate about teaching creationism and evolution in schools in the United States, the question of faith schools in the UK,[1] and, perhaps most of all, the popular perception of Christianity as unscientific (or even antiscientific) because of the Genesis account – a perception that has been vocally endorsed by the New Atheists, although their influence is waning.

I once met a literature professor from a famous university in a country where it was difficult to discuss the Bible publicly. She was intrigued to learn that I was an academic who took the Bible seriously, and said that she would like to ask me something she had never dared to ask. She also said, with typically Eastern sensitivity, that she was reluctant in case her question would offend me: "We were taught at school that the Bible starts with a very silly, unscientific story of how the world was made in seven days. What do you have to say about it as a scientist?"

This book has people like her in mind, who have been reluctant to even consider the Christian faith for this kind of reason. It is also written for the many convinced Christians who are disturbed, not only by controversy over the biblical creation account, but also by the fact that even those who take the Bible seriously do not agree on its interpretation. For instance, some people think that the only faithful interpretation is the young-earth, literal view of the Genesis days that was made famous by Archbishop Ussher (1581–1656) of the city of Armagh in Northern Ireland – where, incidentally, I lived for the first eighteen years of my life. Ussher gave 4004 BC as the date for the origin of the earth. His calculation, based on taking the days of Genesis 1 as twenty-four-hour days of one earth week at the beginning of the universe, is six orders of magnitude away from the current scientific estimate of around four billion years.

Others hold that the text can be understood in concord with contemporary science. Such old-earth creationists are, like their young-earth counterparts, split, some accepting Darwin's theory of evolution as valid, and others not. Finally, still others argue that the Genesis account is written to communicate timeless theological truth rather than scientific information, so that attempts to harmonize it with science are misguided.

The topic is clearly a potential minefield. Yet I do not think that the situation is hopeless. For a start, many Christians, like me, are convinced of the inspiration and authority of Scripture and have spent their lives actively engaged in science and mathematics. We think that since God is the author both of his Word the Bible and of the universe, there must ultimately be harmony between correct interpretation of the biblical data and correct interpretation of the scientific data. Indeed, it was the conviction, based squarely on Genesis 1, that there was a creative intelligence behind the universe and the laws of nature that gave the prime stimulus and momentum to the modern scientific quest to understand nature and its laws in the sixteenth and seventeenth centuries. Furthermore, science, far from making God redundant and irrelevant, as atheists often affirm, actually confirms his existence, which is the theme of my book *Cosmic Chemistry*.[2]

ORGANIZATION OF THE BOOK

This book has five chapters and four appendices. As an introduction to controversy and how we handle it, the first chapter discusses the challenge which the scientific theory that the earth was moving in space posed to generally accepted biblical interpretation in the sixteenth century. The second chapter deals with basic principles of biblical interpretation and applies them to that controversy. The third chapter is the heart of the book, where we consider the interpretation of the Genesis days. The fourth is given over to the biblical account of the origin of human beings, their antiquity, and related theological questions about death. Finally, in the fifth chapter we balance our discussion of the creation week by drawing on the New Testament in order to learn what aspects of the Genesis 1 creation narrative are emphasized there, and why they are relevant for us today.

The appendices deal with several issues that, though important, are placed at the end of the book so that the reader can engage with the main biblical material without many digressions. Appendix A looks at the background of Genesis in terms of culture and literature. Appendix B describes the convergence of Genesis and science over the beginning. Appendix C considers the question of whether there is conflict between Genesis 1 and Genesis 2. Finally, appendix D considers theistic evolution, with special attention paid to so-called "God of the gaps" arguments.

I would like to emphasize that this little book does not pretend to be exhaustive in its scope. It has been written in response to frequent requests over the years. In order to keep it short, I have had to prioritize those issues about which I have been questioned most often. Many other interesting issues have had to be omitted.

NOTES

1. These are confessional schools of Jewish, Christian, Muslim, or any other religious foundation.

2. John C. Lennox, *Cosmic Chemistry: Do God and Science Mix?* (Oxford: Lion Hudson, 2021).

CHAPTER 1

BUT DOES IT MOVE?

A Lesson from History

This book deals with a very controversial topic. There is a certain irony about it, since there would be little controversy if we only possessed the New Testament (NT) and not the Old Testament (OT) as well, as is the case in many less privileged parts of the world. If that were the case, we would know that there had been a beginning and that the world had been created by the Word of God. But we never would have heard of the seven days. So it might be a good thing, before plunging into the nitty-gritty of this book, if you, the reader, paused to reflect on what you would believe about creation if you had never seen the OT.

At times, disagreement about the interpretation of the Genesis narrative of creation has been rather acrimonious. However, even though I am Irish, I am not going to suggest that the best way to approach it is to have a good fight! Indeed, in order to get some kind of perspective on the way we handle controversy, we shall consider another controversy, one that arose in the sixteenth century. If I had been writing a book like this at that time, I might well have been addressing the question: What are we to think of astronomer Nicolaus Copernicus's suggestion that the earth moves, when Scripture seems to teach that it is fixed in space?

Would that topic set your pulse racing? I suspect not. Yet only a few centuries ago, it was a very hot-button issue. The reason? In the fourth century BC the famous Greek philosopher Aristotle had taught that the earth was fixed in the centre of the universe and that the sun, stars, and planets revolved around it[1] – although it is interesting to learn that Aristarchus of Samos (d. 230 BC), a Greek astronomer and mathematician, early as 250 BC had proposed a heliocentric[2] system, even placing the planets in their correct order of distance from the sun. Aristotle's fixed-earth view held sway for centuries. After all, it made a lot of sense to ordinary people: The sun appears to go round the earth; and if the earth moves, why aren't we all flung off into space? Why does a stone, thrown straight up into the air, come straight down if the earth is rotating rapidly? Why don't we feel a strong wind blowing in our faces in the opposite direction of the earth's motion? Surely the idea that the earth moves is absurd, isn't it?

Aristotle's work was translated into Latin, and in the Middle Ages, with the aid of the massive intellect of Thomas Aquinas (1225–1274), it came to influence the church. Aristotle believed not only that the universe was old, but that it had always existed. Aquinas had no difficulty reconciling an eternal universe with the existence of God as Creator in a philosophical sense, but he did admit there was difficulty reconciling that view with the Bible, since the Bible clearly states that there was a beginning. The idea of a fixed earth was different: it seemed to fit in well with what the Bible said. For instance:

> Tremble before him, all the earth;
> yes, the world is established; it shall never be moved.
> *1 Chronicles 16:30*

> Yes, the world is established; it shall never be moved.
> *Psalm 93:1*

> He set the earth on its foundations,
>   so that it should never be moved.
> *Psalm 104:5*

> For the pillars of the earth are the LORD's,
>   and on them he has set the world.
> *1 Samuel 2:8*

Furthermore, the Bible seemed not only to teach that the earth was fixed; it seemed equally clearly to say that the sun moved:

> In them he has set a tent for the sun,
>   which comes out like a bridegroom leaving his
>   chamber,

and, like a strong man, runs its course with joy.
Its rising is from the end of the heavens,
    and its circuit to the end of them,
    and there is nothing hidden from its heat.

Psalm 19:4–6

The sun rises, and the sun goes down,
    and hastens to the place where it rises.

Ecclesiastes 1:5

It is not surprising, therefore, that when Copernicus published his famous work *On the Revolutions of the Celestial Orbs* in 1543, in which he revived Aristarchus's theory with attribution, suggesting that the earth and the planets orbited the sun, his view was called into question by many Protestants and Catholics alike. It is alleged that even before Copernicus published his book (1539), Martin Luther had rejected the heliocentric point of view in rather strong terms in his *Table Talk*:

There is talk of a new astrologer who wants to prove that the earth moves and goes around instead of the sky, the sun, the moon, just as if somebody . . . moving in a carriage or ship might hold that he was sitting still and at rest while the earth and the trees walked and moved. But that is how things are nowadays: when a man wishes to be clever he must . . . invent something special, and the way he does it must needs be the best! The fool wants to turn the whole art of astronomy upside-down. However, as Holy Scripture tells us, so did Joshua bid the sun to stand still and not the earth.[3]

It should be said, however, that many of Luther's comments in *Table Talk* were made tongue in cheek, and there is considerable debate about the authenticity of this quote. Historian John Hedley Brooke writes, "Whether Luther really referred to Copernicus as a fool has been doubted, but in an off-the-cuff dismissal he remembered that Joshua had told the sun, not the earth, to stand still."[4]

John Calvin, on the other hand, believed that the earth was fixed: "By what means could it [the earth] maintain itself unmoved, while the heavens above are in constant rapid motion, did not its Divine Maker fix and establish it?"[5]

Some years after Copernicus, in 1632, Galileo Galilei challenged the Aristotelian view in his famous book *Dialogue concerning the Two Chief World Systems*. This incident has gone down in history as an iconic example of how religion is antagonistic to science. Yet Galileo, far from being an atheist, was driven by his deep inner conviction that the Creator, who had "endowed us with senses, reason and intellect," intended us not to "forego their use and by some other means to give us knowledge which we can attain by them."[6] Galileo held that the laws of nature are written by the hand of God in the "language of mathematics"[7] and that the "human mind is a work of God's and one of the most excellent."[8]

Historian of science Paul Marston gives a fascinating account of Galileo's life, work, and tribulations. His considered view of Galileo is:

> He was a fundamentally proud man, with an inflated idea of his own importance. He was dismissive not only of the ignorant, but of Tycho [Brahe] (as verbose) and even [Johannes] Kepler (as what we might call a 'luney' because he believed the moon caused the tides). Galileo worsened with age – though recurrent illness and a painful hernia may partly explain this. *The Starry Messenger* and *Letters on Sunspots* were fairly polite, *The Assayer* was largely an outburst of unjustified conceit with little of value in it, and his first *Dialogue* treated all opponents (and his friend the Pope) as idiots. His treatment of various Jesuits (particularly [Christoph] Scheiner and [Orazio] Grassi) and Urban VIII probably deserved much greater enmity than he actually received. Other friends could only look on as good prudent advice was ignored and Galileo painted himself (and his church) into a corner.
>
> How should we view the "'trial'? As [Arthur] Koestler said in his classic book [*The Sleepwalkers*], we cannot see it as a kind of "showdown" between enlightened reason and blind faith. Galileo himself never wavered in his Catholic faith; he was advocating science which was at least twenty-four years out of date and had

no proof at all that the Earth moved apart from a bogus one which contradicted his own dynamics.[9]

There is, of course, no excuse whatsoever for the Roman Catholic Church's use of the Inquisition to muzzle Galileo, nor for its subsequently taking several centuries to rehabilitate him. Yet, again contrary to popular belief, Galileo was never tortured, and his ensuing house arrest was spent, for the most part, in luxurious private residences belonging to friends. Furthermore, he clearly brought many of his problems on himself by his lack of tact.

Many historians of science conclude, therefore, that the Galileo affair really does nothing to confirm the simplistic conflict view of the relationship of science to religion.[10]

It took many years thereafter to establish the heliocentric view, which my readers, I presume, now accept, being quite comfortable with the idea that not only does the earth rotate about its own axis, but it moves in an elliptical orbit round the sun at an average of 30 kilometres per second (about 67,000 miles per hour), taking a year to complete the circuit.

But now we need to face an important question: Why do Christians accept this "new" interpretation and not still insist on a "literal" understanding of the "pillars of the earth"? Why are we not still split up into fixed-earthers and moving-earthers? Is it really because we have all compromised and made Scripture subservient to science?

NOTES

1. Often referred to as the Ptolemaic system.

2. *Heliocentric* means "with the sun at the centre," from the Greek *helios*, "sun."

3. Martin Luther, *Table Talk*, quoted in Nicolaus Copernicus, *On the Revolutions of the Heavenly Spheres*, vol. 16 in *Great Books of the Western World* (Chicago: Encyclopedia Britannica, 1952), 497–838.

4. John Hedley Brooke, *Science and Religion: Some Historical Perspectives* (Cambridge: Cambridge University Press, 1991), 96.

5. John Calvin, *Commentary on the Book of Psalms* (Grand Rapids: Eerdmans, 1949), 4:6–7.

6. Galileo Galilei, Letter to the Grand Duchess Christina of Tuscany, 1615, www.wright.edu/~christopher.oldstone-moore/galileo.htm.

7. Galileo Galilei, *The Assayer*, trans. Stillman Drake (1623), https://web.stanford.edu/~jsabol/certainty/readings/Galileo-Assayer.pdf.

8. Galileo Galilei, *Dialogue concerning the Two Chief World Systems*, rev. ed., trans. Stillman Drake (1953; repr., New York: Modern Library, 2001), 120.

9. Paul Marston, *Great Astronomers in European History* (Bristol: Canopus [for University of Central Lancashire], 2014), 229.

10. See John C. Lennox, *Cosmic Chemistry: Do God and Science Mix?* (Oxford: Lion Hudson, 2021), chapter 3.

CHAPTER 2

BUT DOES IT MOVE?

A Lesson about Scripture

HOW SHOULD WE UNDERSTAND THE BIBLE?

The issue at stake in the Galileo controversy is how the Bible should be interpreted. So let us think about some general principles of interpretation before we apply them to the moving-earth controversy.

The first obvious yet important thing to say about the Bible is that it is literature. In fact, it is a whole library of books – some of them history, some poetry, some in the form of letters, and so on, very different in content and style. In approaching literature in general, the first question to ask is, how does the author who wrote it wish it to be understood? For instance, the author of a mathematics textbook does not intend it to be understood as poetry; Shakespeare does not intend us to understand his plays as exact history; and so on.

Next, it make sense that one should *in the first instance*

be guided by the natural understanding of a passage, sentence, word, or phrase in its context – historically, culturally, and linguistically. This was realized a long time ago. In the tenth century Rabbi Saadia Gaon (882–942) wrote: "And so I declare first of all, that it is a well-known fact that every statement in the Bible is to be understood in its literal sense except those that cannot be so construed for one of the following . . . reasons: it may for example, either be rejected by the observation of the senses . . . or else the literal sense may be negated by reason."[1] According to former chief rabbi of the UK, Lord Sacks, "the view of Saadia . . . shared by all the medieval philosophers, is that when a biblical text is incompatible with either reason or observation, this is sufficient evidence that it is to be read figuratively, allegorically, poetically or in some other way. Reason and observation, later to become the methodology of science, were regarded as reliable bases of knowledge, and it was taken as axiomatic that the Torah could not conflict with established truth."[2]

The Christian Reformers, however, were not so happy with allegorical interpretations like, for instance, those of the Jewish writer Philo, who says of the rivers of Genesis: "The four Rivers are the particular Virtues, effluxes of generic Virtue, the River that issues from 'Eden,' which is the Wisdom or Reason of God."[3] To avoid this kind of thing, the Reformers adopted an approach described by the *Oxford English Dictionary* in its definition of *literal* as "that sense or interpretation (of a text) which is obtained by taking its words in their natural or customary meaning, and applying the ordinary rules of grammar; opposed to *mystical, allegorical,* etc.," and "hence, by extension . . . the relatively primary sense of a word, or . . . the sense expressed by the actual wording of a passage, as distinguished from any metaphorical or merely suggested meaning."[4] Of course, there is nothing new in this way of understanding literature. It is what we all use every day in our reading and conversation, without even thinking about it.

The importance of considering the natural understanding of a passage is clear when it comes to the basic teaching of the Christian faith. The crucial thing about Christianity's fundamental doctrines is that they are first and foremost to be understood in their natural, primary sense. The cross of Christ is not a metaphor. It involved an actual death. The resurrection is not a metaphor. It was a physical event: a "standing up again"[5] of a body that had died. However, we know from the Gospels that people listening to Jesus sometimes took him literally when he was speaking metaphorically (in John 6:51, for instance).

But this basic principle needs to be qualified. For instance, when we are dealing with a text that was produced in a different culture distant from our own both in time and in geography, what we think the natural meaning is may not have been the natural meaning for those to whom the text was originally addressed. We shall consider this issue in due course.

At this stage we make a few general remarks about the way we use language. Some of us will be familiar with what I am about to say, but many of us may not have thought much about *how* we use language – we are too busy using it to bother. However, spending just a little time thinking about this matter will help us greatly.

Firstly, there can be more than one natural reading of a word or phrase. For example, in Genesis 1 there are several instances of this. The word *earth* is first used for what we now call the planet, and then a little later it is used for the dry land as distinct from the sea. Both times the word *earth* is clearly meant literally, but the two meanings are different, as is clear from their context.

Next, in many places a literal understanding will not work. Let's take first an example from everyday speech. We all understand what a person means when they say: "The car was flying down the road." The car and the road are very literal, but "flying" is a metaphor. It stands for something real that we could express more literally as "driving fast." Just because a sentence contains a metaphor doesn't mean it is not referring to something real. Indeed, metaphors in general do stand for something real.

For a biblical example, take Jesus' statement "I am the door" (John 10:9). It is clearly not meant to be understood in the primary, literal sense of a door made of wood or any other material. It is intended metaphorically. But notice, again, that the metaphor stands for something real: Jesus is a real means of access into an actual, and therefore very literal, experience of salvation and eternal life. We should also note that the reason we do not take this statement literally has to do with our experience of the world. We know about doors, and our experience with them tells us that Jesus is using a metaphor. We shall return to this point later.

Furthermore, it is impossible, as C. S. Lewis pointed out, to speak of things beyond our immediate senses without using metaphor.[6] Scientists, therefore, use metaphor all the time. They talk about light particles and wave packets of energy, but they don't intend you to imagine light as literal tiny balls, or energy as literal waves on the sea. Yet in each case the metaphor is describing something real – literal if you like – at a higher level.

To make things more complicated but also more interesting, sometimes both a primary and a metaphorical sense can occur together. Take the ascension of Jesus, for example. In its primary sense it refers to the literal, vertical ascent of Jesus into the sky that was physically observed by the disciples.[7] However, there is more to it than that. The literal upward movement carries a deeper meaning – he ascended to the throne of God. For instance, Queen Elizabeth II acceded to the throne of England on the death of her father in 1952 and was subsequently crowned in 1953. When we describe that whole process as ascending the throne, we do not simply mean her act of climbing up onto an ornate chair in Westminster Abbey. She did that, of course; but that (literal) getting up on the chair was at the same time a metaphor or symbol of her (literal) assumption of real power over her people. Similarly, the (literal) ascension of Jesus is a metaphor for his (literal) assumption of universal authority.

Not only do we find metaphor in Scripture, as in most literature, but we also find other figures of speech, such as allegory, for example. Think of Paul's language in Galatians 4:24–26:

> Now this may be interpreted allegorically: these women are two covenants. One is from Mount Sinai, bearing children for slavery; she is Hagar. Now Hagar is Mount Sinai in Arabia; she corresponds to the present Jerusalem, for she is in slavery with her children. But the Jerusalem above is free, and she is our mother.

Hagar was a "literal" woman. Here Paul uses her in an allegory; that is, he imposes a symbolic meaning that has nothing directly to do with the original historical context. So, in this passage, she is both literal and allegorical. We need also to be clear that metaphor and allegory are not the same thing, so that, in particular, the use of metaphor in an account of historical events does not mean the account is allegorical. For a thorough and very informative investigation of how the New Testament uses the Old Testament and how we should interpret the latter in general, *The Riches of Divine Wisdom* by David Gooding is highly recommended.[8]

The examples given above show that the Bible, like all great literature, is replete with figures of speech. It is common nowadays to reserve the word *literalistic* for the basic, primary meaning of a word or expression, and *literal* is often used for the natural reading as intended by the author or speaker.

Thus, reading the phrase "the car was flying down the road" in a literalistic way would mean understanding the car to be actually flying. Reading it "literally," that is, in the natural sense, would mean that the car was going very fast. However, this usage of *literal* is not agreed on by all, which often leads to confusion. We must, therefore, be very careful (and sparing) with our use of *literal*.

I recall once talking about the Genesis creation narrative with a well-known astrophysicist, who suggested to me that it was primitive to believe the Bible. To illustrate a point, I wrote on his blackboard: "And God said, Let there be light. And there was light." He said: "That sounds really primitive. You don't really believe it, do you? It suggests that God has a physical voice box and speaks like we do." In other words, my colleague was taking the word *said* in its primary, natural, human sense – he was taking it literalistically. I laughed and told him that it was now he who was being primitive. Of course God, who is spirit, doesn't have a physical voice box, but he *can* communicate. In other words, the expression "and God said" denotes real, literal communication, but we do not have the slightest idea as to how it is done.

The word *said* means something different for God than it does for us,[9] but the two usages are sufficiently related for one word to work at both the literal and the metaphorical levels. The reason I was amused when my astrophysicist friend made his remarks is that, as I reminded him, scientists use metaphors all the time without batting an eyelid. They, of all people, should not complain when the Bible uses them.

I did not tell my astrophysicist friend at the time that I was essentially quoting Basil the Great, an influential theologian from the fourth century: "When we speak of a voice and a word and a command with reference to God, we mean the divine word, not a sound sent out through phonetic organs."[10]

A helpful general point about language was made by Henri Blocher: "Human speech rarely remains at the zero point of plain prose, which communicates in the simplest and most direct manner, using words in their ordinary sense."[11] We all use metaphors in our ordinary conversation. How colorless life would be without them!

More could be said about the use of language, but perhaps we now have enough to grasp the basic idea. And I am sure the last thing the reader wants is for this book to turn into a lengthy lesson in grammar!

It would be a pity if, in a desire (rightly) to treat the Bible as more than a book, we ended up treating it as less than a book by not permitting it the range and use of language, order, and figures of speech that are (or ought to be) familiar to us from our ordinary experience of conversation and reading.

If we take into account our experience of language, the answer to the question as to at what level a text should be read is often obvious. We use our common sense. We start by taking the natural, primary, base-level literal meaning; and if that doesn't make sense, we go for the next level, which involves metaphor – for example, Jesus' statements "I am the door" (John 10:9) and "I am the bread of life" (John 6:48).

But there are instances where the answer does not seem to be so obvious, in the sense that believers in all ages who are fully convinced of the authority of Scripture come up with different interpretations. What should we do in such a situation? That was the pressing issue in the time of Galileo. So let us apply what we have learned to the moving-earth controversy, so that we may see how Christians eventually came to accept this "new" interpretation and ceased to insist on a literalistic understanding of the foundations and pillars of the earth.

Of course, this did not happen overnight. For many years, if not centuries, one can imagine there being two major polarized positions: the fixed-earthers and the moving-earthers, with the latter group growing in number all the time. These positions were held, not only by people for whom Scripture had little or no authority (although there must have been some such), but by those who were convinced that the Bible was the inspired Word of God and who regarded it as the full and final authority. The latter would agree on the core elements of the gospel, including the doctrines of creation; the fall; salvation; the incarnation, life, death, burial, resurrection, and ascension of Jesus; the expectation of his return; and the final judgement. They disagreed, however, on what Scripture taught about the motion of the earth.

This immediately raises several questions. Were these differences driven simply by a desire on the part of the moving-earth faction to fit in with advances in science, or were they the result of intransigence and antiscientific attitudes on the part of the fixed-earth faction? Did the moving-earthers necessarily compromise the integrity and authority of Scripture?

THE BIBLE AND SCIENCE

First, some general comments. It is often said that the Bible is not relevant to science at all. Indeed, well-known American paleontologist Stephen Jay Gould of Harvard University suggested that religion and science belong to separate domains or *magisteria*.[12] By this he meant that science and religion deal with fundamentally distinct questions, and harmony can be achieved if we keep the two completely apart.

Now this view, often referred to by the acronym NOMA (**N**on-**O**verlapping **MA**gisteria), has an obvious attraction since, if science and the Bible have nothing to do with each other, we can relax – problem solved. However, there are two big snags. Firstly, the claim that science and religion are completely separate often conceals the assumption that science deals with reality, and religion with things like Santa Claus, the Tooth Fairy, and God. The impression that science deals with truth, whereas religion deals with fantasy, is widespread. No one who is convinced of the truth, inspiration, and authority of Scripture could agree with that.

But there is another snag with Gould's view. We cannot keep science and Scripture completely separate, for the simple reason that the Bible talks from time to time about some of the things that science talks about. And these are very important things, such as the origin of the universe and of life. They are also foundational to science, philosophy, and theology. "In the beginning, God created the heavens and the earth" (Genesis 1:1) and "God created man in his own image" (Genesis 1:27) are statements about the objective physical universe and the status of human beings, with far-reaching implications for our understanding of the universe and of ourselves. Whatever else the creation narrative is, it is an account of the creation of the physical universe.

Let me make my position clear. I am a scientist who believes Scripture to be the Word of God. I am not shy, therefore, about drawing scientific implications from it, where warranted. However, saying that Scripture has scientific implications does not mean the Bible is a scientific treatise from which we can deduce Newton's laws, Einstein's equations, or the chemical structure of common salt. John Calvin wrote in his commentary on Genesis: "Nothing is here treated of but the visible form of the world. He who would learn astronomy, and other recondite arts, let him go elsewhere."[13]

Indeed, one of the fascinating tasks we are encouraged to do in God's universe is to find out many things for ourselves. For example, the great seventeenth-century Christian naturalist John Ray did precisely that. Remember, according to Genesis, it was God himself who told the first humans to name the animals; he was not going to do it for them

(Genesis 2:19–20). That is important, because naming things is the very essence of science (we call it *taxonomy*). Indeed, naming things is an essential part of all intellectual disciplines. So we might say that it was God who started science off! It was for this reason that the brilliant scientist James Clerk Maxwell had the words of Psalm 111:2 (KJV) engraved on the Cavendish Laboratory in Cambridge: "The works of the LORD are great, sought out of all them that have pleasure therein." God loves an enquiring mind, a fact that has been a great encouragement to me in my study of mathematics and the history and philosophy of science – and everything else.

We can surely also agree that the Bible is not written in contemporary scientific language. This circumstance should not cause us any surprise or difficulty, but rather gratitude and relief. Suppose, for instance, that God had intended to explain the origin of the universe and life to us in detailed scientific language. Science is constantly changing, developing, standing in need of correction, although (we trust) becoming more and more accurate. If the biblical explanation were at the level, say, of twenty-second-century science, it would likely be unintelligible to most people, maybe even including scientists today. This could scarcely have been God's intention. He wished his meaning to be accessible to all.[14] Indeed, one of the most remarkable things about Genesis is that it is accessible to, and has a message for, everyone, whether or not they are scientifically literate. As John Calvin put it, "The Holy Spirit had no intention to teach astronomy; and, in proposing instruction meant to be common to the simplest and most uneducated persons, he made use by Moses and the other prophets of popular language . . . The Holy Spirit would rather speak childishly than unintelligibly to the humble and unlearned."[15] This statement, be it noted, does not come from someone who was vague about the authority of Scripture; nor is it a recent reflection produced by the alleged embarrassment of Christians confronted by modern science. Indeed, Augustine (AD 354–430) had already had the same thought a thousand years before Calvin: "Nowhere in the Gospel do we read that the Lord said: 'I am sending you a Paraclete[16] who will teach you about the course of the sun and the moon.' For he wanted to make Christians, not mathematicians."[17] Well, as a Christian mathematician myself, I am not sure that those two groups are mutually exclusive, but I take Augustine's point in the spirit in which he intended it.

Rather than scientific language, the Bible often uses what is called *phenomenological* language, the language of appearances. It describes what anyone can see, such as the sun *rising*. Even scientists do this, though they know that the sun only appears to rise because of the rotation of the earth. Saying that the sun "rises" does not commit the Bible, or a scientist for that matter, to any particular model of the solar system.

Having said all that, however, I must once again emphasize the key issue. The Bible, though not a scientific text, precisely because it is God's revealed Word, has *truth* to tell us about the same kind of objective reality that science discusses, in particular about the nature and origin of the cosmos and of human beings. We therefore must try to understand that truth. But it has more than that to say at another level, for instance, truth about the meaning of the universe, which science does not and cannot provide. As Rabbi Jonathan Sacks said: "The meaning of the system lies outside the system."[18]

In that connection it is helpful to reflect on a comment made in *Biblical Interpretation in the Early Church* by Lutheran writer Karlfried Froehlich:

All early Christian interpreters of Scripture operated with the understanding that biblical texts generally have a literal sense and can also convey a higher or spiritual meaning. No great intellectual effort went into recognizing that Scripture has a literal sense. In most cases, some meaning presented itself to the interpreter as the obvious one, and this was taken to be the literal meaning. Unlike today, pride of place was not given to the literal sense. Consequently, there was little motivation to establish a precise definition of "literal." Expressions used to describe this basic sense include "according to the letter," "on the surface," "the obvious meaning," "the proper sense," "what is evident from the text," and "words used for what they were invented to signify." In reality, there is no clear concept of "literal" interpretation that is shared by all early Christian exegetes, and one cannot even assume that an individual author is entirely consistent in usage.[19]

Augustine wrote a treatise titled *On the Literal Meaning of Genesis*. As we have already indicated, his use of the term *literal* in the title is different from our normal usage. The *Stanford Encyclopedia of Philosophy* explains: "'Literal' does not mean 'literalist' but denotes the hermeneutic assumption that the text is really about the creation of the world (as opposed to a moralist or prophetic allegorical reading of the kind proposed in Augustine's early *De Genesi contra Manichaeos*; the two approaches are compatible because Augustine, like Origen and the Jewish exegete Philo before him, believes in the existence of multiple layers of meaning in Scripture)."[20]

In this book, Augustine offered Christians some valuable advice on how to engage with science. It shows that our scientifically advanced era is not the first one to be aware of the tension precipitated by a perceived conflict between science and the biblical record. Augustine was well acquainted with it in his own day.[21] What he has to say is worth quoting at some length in order to capture its spirit:

> Usually, even a non-Christian knows something about the earth, the heavens . . . and this knowledge he holds to as being certain from reason and experience. Now, it is a disgraceful and dangerous thing for an infidel to hear a Christian, presumably giving the meaning of

Holy Scripture, talking nonsense on these topics; and we should take all means to prevent such an embarrassing situation, in which people show up vast ignorance in a Christian and laugh it to scorn . . . If they find a Christian mistaken in a field which they themselves know well and hear him maintaining his foolish opinions about our books, how are they going to believe those books in matters concerning the resurrection of the dead, the hope of eternal life, and the kingdom of heaven, when they think their pages are full of falsehoods and on facts which they themselves have learnt from experience and the light of reason?[22]

Augustine has put his finger on one of the reasons few, if any, of us would maintain a base-level literalistic interpretation of the foundations and pillars of the earth. We just don't wish to appear scientifically illiterate and thus bring the Christian message into disrepute. Of course, but it needs to be said, Augustine is not suggesting that Christians should not be prepared to face ridicule over fundamental doctrines of the Christian message, such as the deity of Christ, his resurrection, and so on. Such ridicule, often based on the false notion that science has made it impossible to believe in miracles,[23] has been evident from the very beginnings of Christianity and still occurs today, as the present author has cause to know.

The take-home message from Augustine is, rather, that if my views on something not fundamental to the gospel – something on which equally convinced Christians disagree – attract ridicule and therefore disincline my hearers to listen to anything I have to say about the Christian message, then I should be prepared to entertain the possibility that it might be my interpretation that is at fault.

Most of us would accept that it is important to distinguish between matters that belong to the core message of the Bible and issues that are less central, where there is room for variation in opinion.[24] We would also accept that we should be prepared to distinguish between what Scripture actually says and what we think it means. It is Scripture that has the final authority, not our understanding of it. It is a sad spectacle that brings discredit on the Christian message when we see those who profess that message belie their profession by fighting among themselves or caricaturing others rather than engaging in respectful discussion, through which all sides just might learn something.

In connection with the motion of the earth, we accept Augustine's advice because we can now see that, although the Bible texts *could* be understood to support a fixed earth, there is a *reasonable alternative* interpretation of those texts that makes far more sense in light of our greater understanding of how the solar system operates.

We know now that the earth does not rest on literal foundations or pillars made of stone, concrete, or steel. We therefore can see that the words *foundations* and *pillars* are used in a metaphorical sense. However, it needs to be emphasized once more that the metaphors stand for realities. God the Creator has built certain very real stabilities into the planetary system that will guarantee its existence so long as is necessary to fulfil his purposes. Science has been able to show us that the earth is stable in its orbit over long periods of time, thanks in part to the inverse square law of gravity; to the presence of the moon, which stabilizes the tilt of earth's axis; and to the existence of the giant planet Jupiter, which helps keep the other planets in the same orbital plane.[25] Earth's stability, therefore, is very real. It is, if you wish, a literal or true stability, even though it does not make sense to understand the word *stability* literalistically as referring to standing motionless.

But there is something more. We also accept the metaphorical interpretation because we can see that it is a perfectly sensible and informed understanding of the biblical text. The earth does not have to be at the centre of the physical universe in order to be a centre of God's attention. Even though our interpretation relies on scientific knowledge, it does not compromise the authority of Scripture. And this is the important point. Scripture has the primary authority. Experience of the world in general and science in particular has helped decide among the possible interpretations that Scripture allows.

Christians are therefore perfectly happy nowadays with a metaphorical interpretation of the foundations and pillars of the earth. They do not regard it as contrived or subservient to science, even though science has helped them refine and adjust their interpretation.

What, then, should we think of the believers of earlier generations who, for hundreds of years, interpreted the biblical record in terms of a fixed earth? Would we accuse them of not believing the gospel and Scripture just because they did not know what we now know? Of course not. For them that interpretation made sense of Scripture and fitted in with the best science of the day. Indeed, no one in the ancient world had clear evidence that the earth moved (although some, like Aristarchus of Samos, had suggested it).

Regarding the attitudes of Martin Luther and John Calvin, John Hedley Brooke is insightful: "The important point is not whether Luther and Calvin happened to make peremptory remarks, exuding a lifetime's confidence in a pre-Copernican cosmology, but whether their exegetical principles implied an inevitable clash as the new system gained in plausibility."[26] And Brooke suggests they did not.

Interestingly, the first hard evidence that the earth moved was not found until 1725, when James Bradley, Savilian Professor of Astronomy at Oxford and later Astronomer Royal, deduced it from his observation of the aberration of the star Gamma Draconis.[27] The earlier Christian interpretation of Scripture in terms of a fixed earth did not attract the ridicule of nonbelievers, since Aristotle's fixed earth had been a widespread view at the time. For many centuries most people never even bothered to question it, because there was no reason to do so.

However, once it became generally evident and accepted that the earth did move, and that the Scriptures could be interpreted consistently with that fact without compromising their integrity or authority, thereafter to maintain that Scripture insisted the earth was fixed in the sky would leave one open to justifiable ridicule and would bring Scripture into disrepute.

FINAL LESSONS FROM GALILEO

The Galileo incident, therefore, teaches us we should be humble enough to distinguish between what the Bible says and our interpretations of it. The biblical text just might be more sophisticated than we first imagined, and we therefore might be in danger of using it to support ideas that it never intended to convey. The Bible *could be* understood to say that the earth is literally fixed in space. But it *does not have to be* understood that way. At least, so Galileo thought in his day, and history has subsequently proved him right.

Philosophers and scientists today also have need of humility in light of facts, even if those facts are being pointed out by a believer in God! Lack of belief in God is no more a guarantee of scientific orthodoxy than is belief in God. What is clear is that criticism of a reigning scientific paradigm[28] may be fraught with risk, no matter who engages in it.

Finally, we see two extremes that must be avoided, although that is often easier said than done. Science is liable to change, and so it may be risky to tie interpretation of Scripture too closely to the science of the day, as the fixed-earthers did, even though, as we have seen, it is hard to blame them in light of the fact that this view was then the reigning *scientific* paradigm. Indeed, it is for this reason that I prefer to speak of the *convergence* between interpretations of Scripture and science at a particular time – for example, the current convergence that there was a beginning, which we shall consider in due course.

The opposite danger is to ignore science, and maybe even common sense. This, as Augustine warned, brings the gospel into disrepute. It is also an obscurantist attitude that finds no support in Scripture. In Romans 1:20, Paul, speaking about God, writes: "For his invisible attributes, namely, his eternal power and divine nature, have been clearly perceived, ever since the creation of the world, in the things that have been made. So they are without excuse." If, therefore, we can learn things about God as Creator from the visible universe, it is surely incumbent upon us to use our God-given minds to think about what these things are, and thus to relate God's general revelation in nature to his special revelation in his Word, so that we can rejoice in both. After all, it was God who put the universe there, and it would be very strange if we had no interest in it.

Finding a balance is not always easy, but we seem to have managed it over the issue of the motion of the earth, even though it only took about seventeen hundred years to get there! I sincerely hope this means there is hope for us on other controversies. We are about to consider one right now.

NOTES

1. *Sefer Emunot ve-Deot*, book VII; quoted in Rabbi Jonathan Sacks, *The Great Partnership: Science, Religion, and the Search for Meaning* (2011; repr., New York: Schocken, 2012), 353.

2. Sacks, *Great Partnership*, 353.

3. Philo, "Allegorical Interpretation of Genesis 2, 3," in *On the Creation*, vol. 1, Loeb Classical Library (Cambridge, MA: Harvard University Press, 1981), 142.

4. *The Compact Edition of the Oxford English Dictionary* (Oxford: Oxford University Press, 1971), s.v., "literal." This is often called the "literal method." We shall discuss the use of the word *literal* below.

5. This is the meaning of the Greek word *anastasis*, used in the New Testament for "resurrection."

6. See C. S. Lewis, *Miracles: How God Intervenes in Nature and Human Affairs* (1947; repr., New York: Macmillan, 1978), 72.

7. See Acts 1, written, it should be observed, by the historian Luke, who, as a doctor, had the nearest approximation to a scientific education of any of the New Testament writers. For Luke's appreciation of the questions arising in connection with science and miracle, see David W. Gooding, *According to Luke: A New Exposition of the Third Gospel* (Leicester, UK: Inter-Varsity, 1987), 37–45. For a scientific viewpoint, see John C. Lennox, *Gunning for God: Why the New Atheists Are Missing the Target* (Oxford: Lion Hudson, 2011), 165–86.

8. David Gooding, *The Riches of Divine Wisdom: The New Testament's Use of the Old Testament* (Coleraine, N. Ireland: Myrtlefield House, 2013).

9. Indeed, when God speaks to certain people in the Bible, he uses human language, though how he does so is, of course, unknown to us. One might go even further and say that God's speech is the primary kind and that human speech is derivative, in the sense that we are made in God's image.

10. Basil, *Exegetical Homilies*, Homily 2, in *The Fathers of the Church*, ed. Roy Joseph Deferrari (Washington, DC: Catholic University of American Press, 1963), 32.

11. Henri Blocher, *In the Beginning: The Opening Chapters of Genesis* (Leicester, UK: Inter-Varsity, 1984), 18.

12. A *magisterium* is a body of teaching; see Stephen Jay Gould, "Nonoverlapping Magisteria," *Natural History* 106 (March 1997): 16–22, www.blc.arizona.edu/courses/schaffer/449/Gould%20Nonoverlapping%20Magisteria.htm.

13. John Calvin, *Commentaries on the First Book of Moses, Called Genesis*, trans. John King (Grand Rapids: Eerdmans, 1988), 1:79.

14. We might also note that biblical Hebrew has a vocabulary of fewer than four thousand words, whereas in English roughly two hundred thousand words are in current use.

15. John Calvin, *Commentary on the Book of Psalms*, vol. 6 (1509; repr., Grand Rapids: Baker, 2009), 104–05.

16. *Paraclete* comes from the Greek word for "one called alongside to help," used of the Holy Spirit in John 15:26.

17. Augustine, *A Debate with Felix the Manichean* (1.10), in *The Faith of the Early Fathers*, vol. 3, ed. William A. Jurgens (Collegeville, MN: Liturgical Press, 1979), 88.

18. Sacks, *Great Partnership*, 9.

19. Karlfried Froehlich, *Biblical Interpretation in the Early Church* (Minneapolis: Fortress, 1980), xxi–xxii, http://ms.augsburgfortress.org/downloads/9781451496376Introduction.pdf.

20. Christian Tornau, "Saint Augustine," in *The Stanford Encyclopedia of Philosophy* (Summer 2020 edition), ed. Edward N. Zalta, https://plato.stanford.edu/archives/sum2020/entries/augustine.

21. Please note that I don't mean a twenty-four-hour day here – but more about that later!

22. Augustine, *The Literal Meaning of Genesis*, vol. 1, in *Ancient Christian Writers: The Works of the Fathers in Translation*, ed. Johannes Quasten, Walter J. Burghardt, and Thomas Comerford Lawler (Mahwah, NJ: Paulist, 1982), 42–43.

23. See John Lennox, *Cosmic Chemistry: Do God and Science Mix?* (Oxford: Lion Hudson, 2021), chapter 6.

24. Of course there will often be differences of opinion as to what is central and what is peripheral.

25. From a mathematical point of view, there are some chaotic elements in the dynamics of the planets. We cannot predict accurately where they will be situated in 100 million years' time, because we cannot measure them accurately enough now. However, these chaotic elements appear to be bounded.

26. John Hedley Brooke, *Science and Religion* (Cambridge: Cambridge University Press, 1991), 96–97.

27. Gamma Draconis is a star that passes directly overhead in London. Bradley detected an annual variation in the apparent position of stars that was due to changes in the earth's velocity. Such calculations led to an estimate for earth's orbital velocity of 30 kilometres per second.

28. A paradigm is a big picture or framework within which science is done.

CHAPTER 3

BUT IS IT OLD?

The Days of Creation

INTERPRETATION OF THE GENESIS DAYS: A BRIEF HISTORICAL PERSPECTIVE

Christians who believe that the "days" in Genesis are, in some sense, sequential periods of time are divided into three basic groups. There are those who take them to be the twenty-four-hour days of one earth week, and who therefore believe that the universe is young (created around six thousand years ago). Then there are others who believe that the days are long periods of time, and that the universe is ancient. Finally, there are those who think that the days are neither literal nor long periods of time, nor even necessarily sequential, but rather schematic. It is important to take on board right away that all of these views go back a very long way. None of them is a recent invention.

The word *creationist*, however, has itself changed in meaning over time. Originally, it meant simply someone who believed in a creator, without any implication for how or when the creating was done; nowadays, confusingly, *creationist* is usually taken to mean "young-earth creationist."[1]

Through the ages many have held that straight lines can be drawn from the creation week of Genesis to the week of ordinary life. The Jewish calendar, for instance, has for centuries taken as its starting point the "Era of Creation," which it dates to 3761 BC (e.g., 2020 was the Jewish year 5780, which ran from September 2019 to September 2020). Furthermore, in contemporary Hebrew, the days of the week are denoted by the numbers 1–6, with the seventh day being Shabbat (= rest) – exactly as in Genesis 1.

The Christian Reformers Martin Luther and John Calvin and many of those who drew up the Westminster Confession would also seem to have held the twenty-four-hour view. In his commentary on Genesis, Calvin said that the duration of creation was "the space of six days," a phrase later adopted into the Westminster Confession.[2]

However, Genesis is the first book in the *Hebrew* Bible, and so the first thing we should do is to go back in history, long before the Reformation, in order to see how Jewish interpreters understood the creation texts. The next step is to see how the early church did so, reading Genesis in the Septuagint Greek version rather than in Hebrew. At this juncture I would like to say that I personally understand the Bible to be a coherent collection of texts emanating from one great Intelligence, that of God the Creator who reveals himself in a manner that is internally consistent and normative for faith and life. It is, therefore, important to see how people of all generations have understood it. Detailed analysis of the entire history of interpretation of Genesis is impossible in a short book, and we shall have to content ourselves with brief sketches.

A very informative account of the history of the Jewish interpretation of Genesis is given by former chief rabbi of the UK Lord Jonathan Sacks in the appendix on Jewish sources on creation, the age of the universe, and evolution in his book *The Great Partnership*.[3] Here are some examples.

Philo (10 BC–AD 50) was an influential Jewish writer who lived in Alexandria at the time of Christ. Among many other works, he wrote a book titled *On the Account of the Creation of the World Given by Moses*. In section 3.13 he said:

> And he [Moses] says that the world was made in six days, not because the Creator stood in need of a length of time (for it is natural that God should do everything at once, not merely by uttering a command, but by even thinking of it); but because the things created required arrangement; and number is akin to arrangement; and, of all numbers, six is, by the laws of nature, the most productive: for of all the numbers, from the unit upwards, it is the first perfect one, being made equal to its parts, and being made complete by them; the number three being

half of it, and the number two a third of it, and the unit a sixth of it.[4]

Thus Philo thought that creation was the act of a moment, and that the Genesis record had more to do with principles of order and arrangement than chronological order. His references to numbers are interesting, as they reflect the Hellenistic "science" of the day – particularly, perhaps, the influence of the Pythagoreans with their fascination with all things numerical. Here is an example showing how Philo expands on day 1: "Now to each of the days He assigned some of the portions of the whole, not including, however, the first day, which He does not even call 'first,' lest it should be reckoned with the others, but naming it 'one' He designates it by a name which precisely hits the mark, for He discerned in it and expressed by the title which He gives it the nature and appellation of the unit, or the 'one.'"[5] Also, Philo took much of the Garden of Eden narrative as symbolic. For instance, in his view, the trees were intended "symbolically rather than literally; for never yet have trees of life or of understanding appeared on the earth, nor is it likely that they will appear hereafter."[6]

The medieval French rabbi Shlomo Yitzchaki (1040–1105), known as Rashi, wrote much-acclaimed commentaries on the Talmud and the Tanakh (Hebrew Old Testament). He did not think that the Genesis creation narrative was proposing either a timescale or even an order for creation: "The text does not intend to point the order of the [acts] of creation . . . the text does not by any means teach which things were created first and which later [it only] wants to teach us what was the condition of things at the time when heaven and earth were created, namely, that the earth was without form and a confused mass."[7]

Maimonides (Moses ben Maimon, 1135–1204) was a Spanish Jewish philosopher and commentator who greatly encouraged the study of science. He wrote:

> What is the way that leads to the love and awe of God? When someone contemplates His great and wondrous works and creatures, and from them obtains a glimpse of His wisdom which is incomparable and infinite, he will immediately love Him, praise Him, glorify Him, and long with an exceeding longing to know his great name, as David said, *My soul thirsts for God, for the living God* (Psalm 42:3). And when he ponders these matters, he will recoil affrighted and realise that he is a small creature, lowly and obscure, endowed with slight and slender intelligence, standing in the presence of Him who is perfect in knowledge. And so David said, *When I consider your heavens, the work of your fingers . . . what is man that you are mindful of him?* (Psalm 8:4–5).[8]

Lord Sacks comments generally on the Jewish attitude towards science: "The sages attached religious dignity and integrity to science, both as human wisdom and as an insight into the divine wisdom evident in the cosmos. The

Babylonian Talmud sees the study of astronomy, for those who are capable of it, as a religious duty. Maimonides sees science as a way to the love and awe of God."[9]

As to interpretation of the creation narratives, Maimonides, in the introduction to his famous work *The Guide for the Perplexed*, modestly said: "Now, on the one hand, the subject of creation is very important, but on the other hand, our ability to understand these concepts is very limited. Therefore, God described these profound concepts, which His Divine wisdom found necessary to communicate to us, using allegories, metaphors and imagery . . . It has been outlined in metaphors so that the masses can understand it according to their mental capacity, while the educated take it in a different sense."[10] He later says: "The account given in Scripture of the creation is not, as is generally believed, intended to be in all its parts literal."[11] This comment would seem to imply that literalistic interpretation was fairly common at the time.

We noted above that the Jewish calendar puts the era of creation at 3761 BC. However, Dov Ginzburg of the Geological Survey of Israel, in his article "The Age of the Earth from Judaic Traditional Literature," shows that there were several views on this. The abstract of his paper says:

> The calculation of the Earth's age, based on ascribing approximately 40 years to each generation mentioned in the Talmud, results in a total of 5,740 years from the "birth" of Adam. For modern scientists holding

traditional viewpoints, this "dating" has led to conflicts which have been explained by various semantic gymnastics. The most common of these is that the Biblical "six days of creation" refers not to days as we know them, but to vast periods of time. However, an examination of the writings of Rabbi Abbahu, Rabbi Abbaye, in the Talmud and Midrash, suggest a concept more akin to our present knowledge. Simon Hahasid in the Talmud estimated the Earth's age as 40,000 years. Based on these early sages, many writers of Jewish religious philosophy in the 10th–12th centuries give ages of the Earth from 50,000 to 100,000 years. Certain Kabbalists from Spain in the 12–13 centuries calculated the Earth's age at 900,000 to 2.5 billion years. A continuation of these concepts are expressed throughout Jewish traditional literature from the Middle Ages to the present by Jewish philosophers and Rabbis such as Maimonides, Rabbi Judah Halevi, Rabbi Israel Lipschitz and others.[12]

In particular, Ginzburg mentions that Rabbi Judah bar Simon in the fourth century pointed out that the Genesis text does not simply say, "It was evening," but *And* it was evening." He deduces that this refers to an earlier time system. Around the same time, Rabbi Abbahu said that this meant God had created and destroyed worlds before the events recorded in Genesis 1, saying: "This one pleases me; those did not please me." The Babylonian Talmud reckoned there were 974 generations before Adam: on the basis of Proverbs 8 they thought that the Torah had existed for a thousand generations before it came to earth through Moses, and since there were twenty-six generations from Adam to Moses, there must have been 974 generations before Adam. In later centuries this view was regarded, for instance, by Rabbi Israel Lipschitz (1782–1860) as being vindicated by geological evidence of an ancient earth and discovery of fossilized remains of extinct animals.[13]

We now turn to the early Christian writers who contributed to what is often called the "Great Tradition" of biblical interpretation. In the second century, some of the early church fathers, such as Justin Martyr (AD 100–165), in his *Dialogue with Trypho*, and Irenaeus, in *Against Heresies*, suggested that the days might have been long epochs, on the basis of Psalm 90:4 ("For a thousand years in your sight are but as yesterday when it is past, or as a watch in the night") and 2 Peter 3:8 ("With the Lord one day is as a thousand years, and a thousand years as one day"). Irenaeus (AD 130–ca. 202) applied this reading of Genesis to the warning God gave regarding the tree of the knowledge of good and evil ("In the day that you eat of it you shall surely die" [Genesis 2:17]). He wrote: "[On] one and the same day on which they ate they also died (for it is one day of the creation) . . . He (Adam) did not overstep the thousand years, but died within their limit."[14]

Clement of Alexandria (AD 150–215) thought that creation could not take place in time at all, since "time was born along with the things which exist."[15] He therefore understood the days to communicate the *priority* of created things but not the *timing* of their creation.

A little later, at the beginning of the third century, Origen (AD 185–254), the most prominent theologian of his time, who lived in Alexandria and was deeply influenced by the Greek practice of allegorical interpretation, said:

> What intelligent person can imagine that there was a first day, then a second and a third day, evening and morning, without the sun, the moon, and the stars? [Sun, moon, and stars are created on the fourth day.] And that the first day—if it makes sense to call it such—existed even without a sky? [The sky is created on the second day.] Who is foolish enough to believe that, like a human gardener, God planted a garden in Eden in the East and placed in it a tree of life, visible and physical, so that by biting into its fruit one would obtain life? And that by eating from another tree, one would come to know good and evil? And when it is said that God walked in the garden in the evening and that Adam hid himself behind a tree, I cannot imagine that anyone will doubt that these details point symbolically to spiritual meanings by using a historical narrative which did not literally happen.[16]

Origen was interested in the fact that in the Genesis account the sun was not made until the fourth day. He made the obvious objection, as we see above: "What intelligent person can imagine that there was a first day, then a second and a third day, evening and morning, without the sun, the moon, and the stars?" We shall consider this objection in the next chapter.

Origen believed that creation was instantaneous and that "the world is not yet ten thousand years old, but very much under that."[17] On the negative side, he was deeply influenced by Plato and believed in the doctrine of pre-incarnate souls for which he was anathematized by the second council of Constantinople in 553, around three centuries after his death. However, it is important also to know that Origen did take the historical level of Scripture seriously. In fact, as influential theologian Henri de Lubac (1896–1991) showed in his book *History and Spirit*,[18] Origen looked for three different levels of interpretation – historical, moral, and mystical-allegorical.[19]

In the fourth century, Basil the Great (AD 330–379), bishop of Caesarea in Cappadocia, gave a series of Lenten lectures called *Hexameron* (Greek for "six days") on the six days of creation. Basil believed that on each day, after God spoke, creation was instantaneous. For example, he wrote: "'Let the earth bring forth grass.' In a moment earth began by germination to obey the laws of the Creator, completed every stage of growth, and brought germs to perfection."[20] Basil also believed that vegetation was created before the sun in order to show that it was not dependent on sunlight, and so the sun should not be worshipped!

Also in the fourth century, Augustine of Hippo (AD 354

−430), a towering intellect who wrote much about Genesis, believed that "God from the start of the ages first created all things simultaneously together, some already in their established natures, some in their pre-established causes."[21] He openly stated in his book *The City of God* that he did not find the days of Genesis easy:

> The world was in fact made *with* time, if at the time of its creation change and motion came into existence. This is clearly the situation in the order of the first six or seven days, in which morning and evening are named, until God's creation was finished on the sixth day, and on the seventh day God's rest is emphasized as something conveying a mystic meaning. What kind of days these are is difficult or even impossible for us to imagine, to say nothing of describing them.
>
> In our experience, of course, the days with which we are familiar only have an evening because the sun sets, and a morning because the sun rises; whereas those first three days passed without the sun, which was made, we are told, on the fourth day. The narrative does indeed tell us that light was created by God ... But what kind of light that was, and with what alternating movement the distinction was made, and what was the nature of this evening and this morning; these are questions beyond the scope of our sensible experience. We cannot understand what happened as it is presented to us; and yet we must believe it without hesitation.[22]

One of the most important statements here from the perspective of philosophical theology is that God did not create "in time" but "with time." That is, according to Augustine, time itself is part of creation, so that the question about what God was doing *before* creation is meaningless. Also, God created *ex nihilo* – out of nothing.

Augustine's final comment here is both honest and humble in that it reminds us there is much in this narrative we don't understand. Yet if we accept that Scripture is the word of God, we should believe it and keep trying to understand it, realizing all the time that we might get it wrong.

In *On the Literal Meaning of Genesis*, Augustine wrote: "But at least we know that it [the Genesis day] is different from the ordinary day with which we are familiar."[23] In fact, he held that God had *created everything in a moment*, and that the days *represented a logical sequence to explain it to us*. We note in passing that Augustine, like Origen, believed in a young earth: "Reckoning by the sacred writings, we find that not 6000 years have yet passed" since the creation of humanity.[24]

These men, we should note, were not armchair theorists. Some of them were tortured or martyred for their faith – among them Justin Martyr (as his name implies), Irenaeus, and Origen. Nor, obviously, were they influenced by contemporary science, such as geology and evolutionary biology. They were also brilliant thinkers, and we must not make the mistake of giving in to what C. S. Lewis called "chronological snobbery"[25] and think that just because we live at a much later time, we must be much more clever by definition.

Hans Boersma points out that "the medieval tradition often distinguished four different levels of interpretation . . . *Littera gesta docet, quid credes allegoria, moralis quid agas, quot tendas anagogia.* In English, one could render the rhyme somewhat freely as follows: *The letter shows us what God and our fathers did; the allegory shows us where our faith is hid; the moral meaning gives us the rule of daily life; the anagogy[26] shows us where we end our strife.*"[27]

In subsequent centuries up to the present time we can trace two main trends in interpretation: a more literal approach, like that of Basil the Great, and a more figurative one, following Augustine. As a member of Oxford University, I must mention Robert Grosseteste (1168–1253) who was a polymath and, in function, if not in title, was chancellor of the University of Oxford. His biographer Robert Southern said of him that he "had come to see that there was no gap between the physics of creation and the theology of creation . . . It was his study of the Bible that convinced him that light was not only the most satisfying of all natural phenomena but also the emanation from the divine nature which at the first moment of creation penetrated and gave form to the whole universe."[28] Of Genesis 1:1 Grosseteste said: "With the hammer of these words Moses crushed the philosophers who assert with Aristotle that the world had no beginning."[29]

He also had two pieces of sensible advice for those who found the understanding of Genesis difficult. The first is that it was not his business to try to settle an issue that had puzzled better men. The second refers to the church fathers and says: "It should be noticed that the holy writers often intend to indicate what was *possible* rather than to assert what *was*, and many of their statements are about possibilities rather than certainties. Even when they seem to us to speak assertively as about absolute truth, they often propound things as an exercise. As Gregory of Nyssa says: 'We put forward what comes into our mind not definitively but as an exercise for our attentive hearers.'"[30] Please bear that in mind as you continue to read what I have written.

One of the major differences in interpretation of the early chapters of Genesis is found between those who think that the author intended the book to be read as history and those who regard the author's intention as the conveying of timeless truths through figurative, theological language.[31] In appendix D we shall consider the effect of Darwin's theory of evolution on the interpretation of Genesis.

I said "the *early* chapters of Genesis," since the impression given by the rest of the book is that of a historical narrative describing the rise of the Hebrew nation from among the Gentile nations of the ancient Near East, and following its chronological development through the family histories of Abraham, Isaac, and Jacob. It is not surprising, then, that many argue that the early chapters of Genesis are a historical narrative, which clearly form an integral part of the book.

However, some, like Gordon Wenham, for instance, suggest that "this chapter stands outside the main historical outline of Genesis, each section of which begins, 'This is the (family) history of . . .'"[32] Still others argue that the first occurrence of this repeated statement *ends* the first section, thus including it in the category of history.

These early chapters of Genesis give me, at least, a strong impression that they are talking about actual things, events, places, and people and give a historical narrative from the creation of the world and the first humans to the development and spread of civilization, down to the time of the great flood through which Noah and his family were preserved to become the progenitors of the nations of the ancient Near East. I sense a potential danger in some quarters of separating theology from history.[33]

Genesis is, of course, a text that comes to us from a time and culture very different from our own – that of the ancient Near East. We cannot, therefore, simply read it as if it were a contemporary Western document written to address contemporary Western concerns.[34]

That raises the question: Just how much was Genesis influenced by the culture in which it was written, and in what sense? This is, of course, a question that can be addressed to any part of the Bible. Those who, like the present author, are convinced that Scripture is God's revelation are also aware that God used human authors who wrote in terms of their own culture and surroundings as they conveyed God's word to the world. Jesus told parables about farming, building, and fishing, not about factories, aviation, and jungle exploration. And yet his parables are accessible to anyone in any age. So it is with Genesis as well. Knowledge of ancient Near Eastern culture can certainly help us a great deal, yet the central statements of Genesis have that timeless quality about them that means they can be understood in 1000 BC or in AD 2000, if read properly.

THE MAIN VIEWS OF THE GENESIS DAYS

The main interpretations of the days of Genesis 1 can be set out as follows:[35]

The 24-hour view	The days are seven 24-hour days, of one earth week, about six thousand years ago.
The day-age view	The days are in chronological order, each representing a period of time of unspecified length.
The framework view	The days exhibit a logical, rather than a chronological, order.

The meanings of the chronological views 1 and 2 are clear; but we shall briefly outline the content of the framework view 3, which is also an ancient interpretation. The basic idea here has to do with the distinction between two kinds of order, to which we referred earlier when we noted that Clement and Augustine thought that the sequence of days in Genesis was a logical rather than a chronological sequence.

An illustration may help us understand the difference between these two kinds of order. If a builder is describing how his company built a hospital, he will probably describe the process chronologically: "We dug a hole, laid foundations, and then put up the superstructure floor by floor: basement, car park; ground floor, administration; first floor, wards; second, operating theatres; third, more wards." But ask the surgeon to describe the construction of the hospital, and he might say: "We put the operating theatre on the second floor and located wards above and below it on the first and third floors." The surgeon describes the hospital logically from his perspective, not chronologically. We are so used to this kind of thing that we take account of it automatically. We certainly would not understand the surgeon to be saying that the operating theatre suddenly appeared in midair and that wards were then constructed above and below it! And yet we would know that the surgeon was describing a very real and literal hospital.

For a biblical example, compare the order given in Genesis 1 with that given in Isaiah 45:12: "I made the earth and created man on it; it was my hands that stretched out the heavens, and I commanded all their host." Would anyone think of deducing from Isaiah that God first created the earth, then humans, and finally the heavens? I think not. Isaiah's semi-poetic description does not prioritize chronology. Nevertheless, let me stress that Isaiah is describing something real – events that really happened – but he is not relating them altogether in the order in which they happened.

The third of the major interpretations in our list, the framework view, prioritizes logical order over chronological and is traceable to the time of the early church fathers.[36] The idea is that the Genesis days form a literary or artistic framework in which days 1–3 form a triad that corresponds to the triad formed by days 4–6:

Day	Forming	Filling	Day
1	Light	Luminaries	4
2	Sky/seas	Sea creatures/ Winged creatures	5
3	Seas/dry land/ vegetation	Land animals/ humans	6

The first triad concerns giving form or structure to what was initially formless, and the second concerns filling the newly created but empty forms. Light, then, is created on day 1, and day 4 tells us about the light bearers: sun, moon, and stars. The creation of the sky and seas occurs on day 2, and on day 5 the sea is filled with sea creatures and the sky with winged creatures.

It has been pointed out that the parallelism is not perfect. For instance, the light bearers of the fourth day are placed in the sky, which is first mentioned on the second day. Hence, if the first and fourth days were truly parallel, the sky would have to exist on the first day. Also, the sea creatures of day 5 belong to the seas of day 3 – or, indeed, to the deep that is mentioned right at the beginning. Nevertheless the parallelism is striking and, furthermore, is of a type found elsewhere in Scripture.[37]

A further variation of view 3 is known as the *cosmic temple view*. According to John Walton, his research on the ancient Near East led him to the view that the days of Genesis 1 form a chronological sequence of twenty-four-hour days but are "not given as the period of time over which the material cosmos came into being, but the period of time devoted to the inauguration of the functions of the cosmic temple, and perhaps also its annual reenactment."[38]

Walton's arguments are based on the unobjectionable observation that we do not today swim in the same "cultural river" as those to whom Genesis 1 was originally addressed, and we need to take that into account to avoid misconstruing the text. I have no quibble with that, and I accept the idea that *one* of the objectives of Genesis 1 is to describe the various functions of the constituents of the universe and their ordering. I am, however, sceptical about the suggestion that this is the only purpose of Genesis 1. Perhaps because of my Irish temperament I would ask: Why not both? It would seem I am not alone in so thinking.[39]

In the framework view, then, the existence of parallels between the first three and the second three days does not necessarily imply that the days do not form a chronological sequence.[40] After all, at the simplest level, you cannot have plants and animals on dry land that does not yet exist. Derek Kidner's comment is apposite: "The march of the days is too majestic a progress to carry no implication of ordered sequence; it also seems over-subtle to adopt a view of the passage which discounts one of the primary impressions it makes on the ordinary reader." However, it should be noted that Kidner also says of the account: "The language is that of every day, describing things by their appearance; the outlines of the story are bold, free of distracting exceptions and qualifications, free also to group together matters that belong together (so that trees, for example, anticipate their chronological place in order to be classified with vegetation), to achieve a grand design in which the demands now of time-sequence, now of subject-matter, control the presentation, and the whole reveals the Creator and his preparing a place for us."[41]

It therefore seems to me at least some degree of *chronological* sequence is intended. The existence of the framework parallels would then indicate that there is *more* to the text than ordered sequence: sequence and framework are not necessarily mutually exclusive. It could just be that a combination of both makes for a better approach.

What then should we think of the different interpretations? Well, the first thing we should note is that they are *different* interpretations of the *same* text. That much is obvious. Secondly, the very fact that they are each held by godly, thoughtful Christians who are agreed on all the central doctrines of Scripture shows us that the interpretation of the days is not a central doctrine. There is room for difference of opinion, and we need to show humility and grace when dealing with those who disagree with us.

We also need to remind ourselves here of an important exegetical principle, which is that we should pay careful attention to *what the text says* before trying to decide *what it means*. This is sometimes easier said than done, since all of us have preconceived ideas. Yet experience shows that problems in interpreting a passage often spring from failing to see exactly what the text says because of impatience to get at the meaning. Of course, in practice it is sometimes difficult to disentangle what we think the text says from what we think it means, but it is nevertheless worth holding the distinction in mind as we proceed. If we believe in the inspiration of Scripture, we must take the text seriously, because it is Scripture that is inspired and not our particular understanding of it, as I said earlier. One way of doing this is to try to read Genesis 1 as if we had never read it before in order to free our minds so far as possible from preconceptions and so come at it fresh.

Let's now look at a table of contents of the first section of Genesis 1:1–2:3:

1. Statement regarding the creation of the heavens and the earth: 1:1–2
2. Six days of God's creation and organizational activity, culminating in the creation of human beings in his image: 1:3–2:1
3. The seventh day, the day of God's rest – Sabbath: 2:2–3

The initial impression is that of a sequence of events, giving the briefest of brief histories of time. The narrative starts with the creation of "the heavens and the earth," that is, the whole show. The shaping and organizing process starts with a world "without form and void" (Genesis 1:2). Then God speaks and through his creative word, step by step, forms and fills the world, until it is eventually fit for habitation by creatures who uniquely bear God's image and likeness – namely, human beings. This movement towards a goal (teleology) accords with the later statement in Isaiah to the effect that God did not create the world empty but created it to be inhabited. That is, emptiness was the initial stage but not the final stage.[42] There were several stages in reaching the goal, each of them seen by God to be good because each of them had fulfilled the purpose God determined for it.

Jewish readers of Genesis 1 in any era would be familiar with that most basic cycle of human life – the working week. They also would have known the law of God in Exodus that refers to the creation narrative: "Remember the Sabbath day, to keep it holy. Six days you shall labor, and do all your work, but the seventh day is a Sabbath to the LORD your God . . . For in six days the LORD made heaven and earth, the sea, and all that is in them, and rested on the seventh day. Therefore the LORD blessed the Sabbath day and made it holy" (Exodus 20:8–11).

Thoughtful readers familiar with the writings of Moses would therefore clearly understand the following: (1) Genesis 1 portrays God as a creative craftsman going about his week of work, taking rest each night from evening to morning and then having a day of rest at the end. (2) Yet God's work of creation was vastly different from human work. We do not do the things that God does. Indeed, the Hebrew word for *create* (*bara*) is used in the Bible mostly with God as subject.[43] (3) Human rest is not the same as God's rest. God does not get tired, as we do – he "neither slumbers nor sleeps" (see Psalm 121:4). (4) God's creation week was never repeated, whereas ours is. Thus there were points of contact between God's creation week and the readers' workweek that they could readily understand, yet there were also differences. The human workweek was similar to God's, but not identical. The question now is, how were the days of God's creation week meant to be understood?

THE MEANING OF THE WORD DAY IN GENESIS 1:1–2:4

1. The Hebrew word *yom*, "day," is first mentioned in Genesis 1:5: "God called the light Day, and the darkness he

called Night." What is the natural reading of this statement? Here day is contrasted with night; so a twenty-four-hour day is *not* in view, but rather "day" in the sense of "daytime" – roughly twelve hours. Compare John 11:9, where Jesus says, "Are there not twelve hours in the day?"[44] The words for *day* in Greek and in English, as well as in Hebrew, have several primary meanings, and "daytime" is one of them.

2. The second time the word for *day* occurs, again in Genesis 1:5, this time "day" involves "evening and morning," so this would naturally be taken to refer to a twenty-four-hour day. So now we have two primary meanings for the word *day* in the same verse.

3. The next occurrence of the word *day* that we need to pay attention to is in the account of the seventh day, the Sabbath, on which God rests from the work of creating. There is no mention here of "evening and morning," as there was for each of the first six days. The omission is striking and calls for an explanation. If, for instance, we ask how long God rested from his work of creation, as distinct from his work of upholding the universe, then Augustine's suggestion – that God sanctified the seventh day by making it an epoch that extends onward into eternity – makes good sense and is one that is followed by many commentators. Thus the seventh day is different from the first six,[45] which are days of creative activity. The sequence of days comes to an end, and God rests from *creation* activity; and he is still resting up to this present day. That is, we are still today in God's Sabbath rest.[46] God is not, however, resting from all activity. In particular, he does not

rest from the work of upholding the universe and the work of salvation and redemption, as implied in Jesus' statement when he was accused of breaking the Sabbath: "My Father is working until now, and I am working" (John 5:17).

It is this conviction – that the seventh day in the Genesis account is a long period of time – that leads some people to think that the other days may similarly indicate long ages. However, caution may be needed here, since as we have just seen, the text itself contains indications that day seven is different from the other six.

4. Finally, in some translations of Genesis 2:4 (NIV and CEV, for instance), we meet the expression "when the LORD God made . . ." In fact, the word *when* is used to translate the Hebrew for "in the day." Clearly the author has no more a twenty-four-hour day in mind here than an elderly man would if he said, "In my young day there were very few aircraft in the sky." He would be using the word *day* quite correctly to describe a period of time, not a particular day of a particular week – as I did earlier in this book when I said, "in Galileo's day." We might compare this use of the word with expressions like "the day of the LORD" and "the last day," which clearly refer to periods of undefined length, and not to twenty-four-hour days.

The word *day*, therefore, has several distinct meanings in the short text of Genesis 1:1–2:4 alone. Each of these meanings is familiar from ordinary usage. They are all natural, primary, literal meanings, each referring to something real and perfectly comprehensible.

A further grammatical point should be made. In many English versions of the Bible, the days of Genesis are rendered as "*the* first day, *the* second day," and so on, each having the definite article. However, even though the Hebrew language does have a definite article (*ha*), it is not used in the original to qualify days one through five. Basil, a fourth-century bishop of Caesarea, thought this was significant: "If then the beginning of time is called 'one day' rather than 'the first day,' it is because Scripture wishes to establish its relationship with eternity. It was, in reality, fit and natural to call 'one' the day whose character is to be one wholly separated and isolated from all the others."[47] Yet, as Old Testament scholar David Gooding has pointed out to me (unpublished), although the Hebrew definite article is not used with the first five days, it is used for days six and seven. A better translation, therefore, would be "day one, day two, day three, day four, day five, *the* sixth day, *the* seventh day"; or, "*a* first day, *a* second day, *a* third day, *a* fourth day, *a* fifth day, *the* sixth day, *the* seventh day."[48]

These then are the facts. The next question is, how should we interpret them? No serious exegete has found this task to be easy, which may mean we simply do not have enough information to be conclusive about some of the details. However, and this is the important thing, we must not let differences at this level deter us from grasping the main message of the narratives.

As we go into more detail, I would like to say that if you imagine I will provide you with the answers to all questions about the seven days, you will be disappointed. I still have many questions of my own. What I wish to do is more modest – namely, to stimulate my readers to think about some *possibilities* and not *certainties*.

THE NATURE OF THE CREATION WEEK

In the three-part structure of Genesis 1:1–2:3 mentioned above, the initial creation act (1:1–2) is separated from the six days of creation that follow it. You will find this structure followed, for instance, in the sectionalizing scheme used in the ESV. The separation between the first two parts is underlined by the fact that there is a change of past tenses between them in the original language. The verb *created* in Genesis 1:1 is in the perfect tense, and "the normal use of the perfect at the very beginning of a pericope[49] is to denote an event that took place before the storyline gets under way."[50] Accordingly, there is a switch to the narrative tense beginning in verse 3. It is therefore linguistically plausible, though admittedly not so obvious, that "the beginning" of Genesis 1:1 was not necessarily intended to be understood as part of day 1, as is frequently assumed. The initial creation could have taken place before day 1, but Genesis does not tell us how long before. Nor does 1:1–2 tell us how long the creation of the heavens and the earth took; indeed, astrophysics would indicate that the "heavens" existed a long time before the earth. This means that the question of the age of the earth (and of the universe) may be a separate question from the interpretation of the days, a point that is frequently overlooked.

In other words, quite apart from any scientific considerations, the text of Genesis 1:1, in separating the beginning from day 1, leaves the age of the universe indeterminate. Sad, therefore, that there has been so much fighting over this issue that has done nothing to commend the rationality and truth of Christianity to a world that isn't remotely interested in such details anyway. It should remind us of the principle that there is always a danger of understanding a text to say less than it does, as well as a danger of making it say more.

The overall situation is beginning to look very similar to that of the fixed-earth controversy. There we saw that, although Scripture *could be* understood as teaching that the earth did not move, it didn't *have to be*. Similarly, although Scripture *could be* understood as teaching that the earth is young, it does not *have to be*.

It is an important principle of Christian interpretation of the Old Testament that we not only consider the text in its own right but also take into account what the New Testament has to say about it. The New Testament does not mention the days of Genesis, let alone comment on their length. Yet it makes a number of important statements on creation that resonate with Genesis 1 – John 1:1, Hebrews 1:3, and Hebrews 11:3, in particular – and emphasize that all things were made by the word of God. That would seem to indicate that one of the main points to be made about the days is contained in the phrase that introduces each of them: "And God said." They each involve a creative or orga-nizational fiat[51] of God's word. Therefore, the fact of what *happens* in each day – God speaks – is much more important than each day's *length*.

That core message is important for our culture: God, the Word, is primary; matter, energy, the universe, and life are derivative. We might say that creation is "word-based." It consists of a sequence of speech acts in each of which God injected a new level of information and energy into what is an open system in order to advance creation to its next level of form and complexity.[52] This, it should be noted, is the exact opposite of a mindless, unguided naturalistic process, Darwinian or otherwise. Not only that, but the idea that information is primary is central to modern physics and biology.[53] More importantly still, since it is word-based, the universe has meaning.

A second important observation about God speaking is that on two of the days God speaks more than once. Days 1 and 2 concern the inorganic world, as does the first men-tion of "And God said" on day 3. However, on day 3 there is a second "And God said" that triggers the origin of life. Thus, and I am wording this carefully, as far as Scripture is concerned, you do not get from the inorganic to the organic without "And God said."

The wording of the second part of day 3 is interesting: "And God said, 'Let the earth sprout vegetation, plants yield-ing seed, and fruit trees bearing fruit in which is their seed, each according to its kind, on the earth'" (Genesis 1:11).

This could imply that God starts life going and allows its potential to develop from there. Think of all the variations on the theme "dog" that have developed, or been bred, originally, probably, from wolves. They did not each require a special "And God said." Also, Paul points out in Acts 17:26 that all the many races, colours, and kinds of humans have arisen by development from the first humans. The point of the repetition of "And God said" in day 3 is to underline that *life did not come from nonlife simply by processes of development.* Life required not only pre-existent matter but also a special creative word of God.

In day 6 a similar thing happens. The first "And God said" leads to the creation of animals, and the second to the creation of human beings. However, there is no suggestion that human beings were made by development out of the animals. According to Genesis, between the existence of animals and that of humans there stands "And God said." It is almost as if the writer of Genesis had foreseen the current debates about the origin of life and the origin of human beings.[54]

Next, to the days themselves. This is where things get more complicated and differences of opinion multiply. If we were listing the days of one normal earth week (in English), we would normally give each of them either the indefinite article or leave articles out altogether. We would not, as Genesis does, omit the definite article for the first five days and supply it for the last two. The presence of the article could indicate that the final two days are special, and we might even imagine why: on the sixth day human beings are made in the image of God, and on the seventh day God rests, his work complete. Both the Jewish writer Philo and the church father Basil noticed this grammatical point, as we saw above, but did not give it the above interpretation. It should be noted that the Septuagint does not have a definite article with day 6. Of course, it could just be that the translators thought it had no special significance, or that they didn't notice it. After all, I have met professors of Hebrew who had not noticed it either!

This grammatical detail may also be a signal to us that the text is more sophisticated than we first might have thought. In particular, it is often assumed that the writer of Genesis intended us to take the days *either* as seven days of one earth week (as in the twenty-four-hour view) *or* as seven time periods of indeterminate length (as in the day-age view) *or* as a logical framework in which to help us picture creation (as in the framework view).

David Gooding suggested years ago that the writer of Genesis may not have intended us to think of the first six days as necessarily days of a single earth week, but rather as a sequence of six *creation* days; that is, days of normal length (with evenings and mornings, as the text says) in which God spoke to inaugurate something new. Such creation days may well have been separated by indefinite periods of time.[55] We have already seen that Genesis arguably separates the initial creation – "the beginning" – from the sequence of days. What Gooding suggested in addition to that is that there may have been time intervals between the days of creation during which the potential of God's stepwise input of information and energy was developed.

This view is clearly consistent with the earth being old, but it raises a number of questions. For example, the sequence in each day is: (1) God speaks; (2) various new things appear; (3) the day closes. If there is anything significant in this order, if this is to be thought of as a twenty-four-hour day, would it not mean, as one critic pointed out to me, that, for example, on day 3 life was created, together with all the many fundamental innovations in vegetation, within the space of twenty-four hours after which nothing happened for a long period? Well, it might, if that is what Gooding was saying, and if so, I agree with the criticism. The idea that just as the seventh day represents an indefinite period of time, so do the first six, would appear to make much better sense than that.

However, I don't think this is what Gooding meant. In private discussion he told me that he thought the spaces between the days involved processes of God's maintenance and development that may have taken geological ages in which not nothing but a great deal happened. Gooding took the days themselves to be about special creative acts that presumably didn't take long but that inaugurated all that happened subsequently. A variation on that theme might be that the days were, in geological terms, comparatively short.

Before we reject this idea, it is worth reflecting that those who believe that all life developed by purely natural

BUT IS IT OLD?

evolutionary processes without special interventions of God – whether unguided, as with the neo-Darwinists, or guided, as with evolutionary creationists (theistic evolutionists) – should not find it difficult to *understand* the idea of God injecting an instantaneous level of information and energy that subsequently takes a long time to develop by "natural" processes, even if they do not *believe* it. Even for them, the first spark of life must have appeared in a moment, certainly less than twenty-four hours, and then that life, once started, subsequently developed its potential without any intervention.

Furthermore, many evolutionary creationists hold that an instantaneous initial creation was front-loaded with all necessary information for life's subsequent development. Gooding suggested that there were several subsequent, instantaneous steps, each front-loaded with what was necessary for the next stage of development. It has to be noted, however, that it is not so easy to reconcile this with the geological record, although Stephen Gould and Niles Eldredge's theory of punctuated equilibrium would seem to go some way towards it.[56]

Also, it seems odd that some I have met who react negatively against this view because it holds that all the significant creative steps occurred in twenty-four-hour periods themselves hold that creation took only a moment. Furthermore, the supernatural acts of Jesus the incarnate Word of God recorded in the New Testament were mainly instantaneous: water is turned into wine without the normal long process; bread and fish are multiplied in an instant. Could not this be intended to show us how the Creator creates?

I can imagine someone objecting to all this by saying that the nature of the days is to be found in a biblical statement already quoted: "Six days you shall labor, and do all your work, but the seventh day is a Sabbath to the LORD your God . . . For in six days the LORD made heaven and earth, the sea, and all that is in them, and rested on the seventh day" (Exodus 20:9–11). Does this not unequivocally mean that the days were all days of a single week?

When I cited this statement from Exodus earlier, I pointed out that there were not only similarities between God's creation week and our workweek, but also obvious differences. God's week happened once; ours is repeated. God's creative activity is very different from ours; God does not need rest as we do; and so on. So it is not possible to draw straight lines from Genesis to our working week. God's week is a pattern for ours, but it is not identical. Thus Exodus 20:9–11 does not *demand* that the days of Genesis 1 be the days of a single week, although it could, of course, be interpreted that way.

In light of this, a Hebrew scholar with a background in science, who was a member of the team of translators of the ESV, C. John Collins, has another way of looking at the days that he calls the "analogical days" view – a view that "takes the word [*day*] in its ordinary meaning, but applies that meaning analogically." He adds, "This is just what we do with other analogical terms like 'eyes of the Lord': we don't need a new entry in the dictionary for 'eye'; we use the ordinary meaning and apply it by analogy to God."[57]

It would be a mistake, of course, to overemphasize the differences between the views expressed in this chapter. No major doctrine of Scripture is affected by whether one believes that the days are analogical days or that each day is a long period of time inaugurated by God's speaking, or whether one believes that each of the days is a normal day in which God spoke, followed by a long period of putting into effect the information contained in what God said on that particular day.[58] What is important is that on each of the days, God spoke – which is not a description of a natural, unguided process.

However, we must not pretend that there are no difficulties with these chronological views.

THE GENESIS ENIGMA

Indeed, it is interesting to see that the correspondence between the sequence given in Genesis and that given by science has been pointed out even by people who set little store by the factual accuracy of the biblical record in passages of this kind. As an example from an earlier era, English philosopher and historian Edwyn Bevan (1870–1943), in an essay titled "The Religious Value of Myths in the Old Testament," writes,

The stages by which the earth comes to be what it is cannot indeed be precisely fitted to the account which modern science would give of the process, but in principle they seem to anticipate the modern scientific account by a remarkable flash of inspiration, which a Christian may also call inspiration.

Supposing we could be transported backward in time to different moments in the past of our planet, we should see it first in a condition in which there was no land distinguishable from the water and only a dim light coming from the invisible sun through the thick volumes of enveloping cloud: at a later moment, as the globe dried, land would have appeared; again at a later moment low forms of life, animal and vegetable, would have begun; sooner or later in the process the cloud-masses would have become so thin and broken that a creature standing on earth would see above him sun and moon and stars; at a still later moment we should see on the earth great primeval monsters; and lastly we should see the earth with its present fauna and flora, and the final product of animal evolution, Man.[59]

Much more recently, Andrew Parker, research director at the Natural History Museum in London, has drawn attention to the same phenomenon in a way that is directly relevant to John Walton's view. Parker, an evolutionary biologist who does not profess to believe in God, was moved to look at Genesis 1 after a number of people had written to him, suggesting that his research on the origin of the eye seemed to echo the statement "Let there be light." He was very surprised at what he found: "Without expecting to find anything, I discovered a whole series of parallels between the creation story on the Bible's first page and the modern, scientific account of life's history. This at least made me think. The congruence was almost exact." He later adds: "The more detail is examined, the more convincing and remarkable I believe the parallels become. One question I will be asking in this book is this: Could it be that the creation account on page one of Genesis was written as it is *because* that is how the sequence of events really happened?"[60] Here is Parker's conclusion:

> Here, then, is the Genesis Enigma: *The opening page of Genesis is scientifically accurate but was written long before the science was known. How did the writer of this page come to write this creation account?* . . . I must admit, rather nervously as a scientist averse to entertaining such an idea, that the evidence that the writer of the opening page of the Bible was divinely inspired is strong. I have never before encountered such powerful, impartial evidence that the Bible is the product of divine inspiration.[61]

It is not surprising that Parker's ideas are hotly contested, particularly by atheists, but his book gives scientific support to the order of events as recorded in Genesis from someone who has no obvious axe to grind.[62]

THE CREATION OF LIGHT AND THE PROBLEMATIC FOURTH DAY

We recall from earlier in this chapter the point that Origen made long ago, which registers with many today. If there is a chronological dimension to the days, how is it that the sun was made on day 4? "And God said, 'Let there be lights in the expanse of the heavens to separate the day from the night . . . and let them be lights in the expanse of the heavens to give light upon the earth.' And it was so" (Genesis 1:14–15). German-American Jewish philosopher Leo Strauss (1899–1973) said of these verses: "The vegetative world was created on the third day and the sun on the fourth day. That is the most massive difficulty of the account given in the first chapter of the Bible."[63]

If the text means that the sun came into existence on day 4, Origen was asking a very reasonable question: If the sun is not yet there, how are we to understand the first three days with their "evenings and mornings'? The word *day* makes no obvious sense in the absence of the sun and the earth's rotation relative to it. In order to overcome this difficulty, some have postulated the existence of a non-solar light source that was created on day 1, corresponding to the cosmological standard model that says that the universe was bathed with light about 240,000 to 300,000 years after the beginning. However, that would, on the one hand, still leave the first three "days" undefined. On the other hand, it would also mean that day 1 introduces light as such, and that could be important.

There is a very interesting paper in the *Proceedings of the Royal Society* titled "A Medieval Multiverse?: Mathematical Modelling of the Thirteenth Century Universe of Robert Grosseteste." The abstract informs us:

> In his treatise on light, written about 1225, Robert Grosseteste describes a cosmological model in which the universe is created in a big-bang-like explosion and subsequent condensation. He postulates that the fundamental coupling of light and matter gives rises to the material body of the entire cosmos. Expansion is arrested when matter reaches a minimum density and subsequent emission of light from the outer region leads to compression and rarefaction of the inner bodily mass so as to create nine celestial spheres, with an imperfect residual core. In this paper, we reformulate the Latin description in terms of a modern mathematical model, teasing out consequences implicit in the text, but which the author would not have had the tools to explore . . . As in current cosmological thinking, the existence of Grosseteste's universe relies on a very special combination of fundamental parameters.[64]

Fascinating – and eight centuries before the Belgian priest and astrophysicist Georges Lemaître proposed the "big bang" scenario in the standard model with which we are familiar today.[65]

An alternative is that day 1 refers to the light of the sun

without naming its source. That makes sense of days 1–6 but creates the obvious problem for day 4. One view, championed by astrophysicist Hugh Ross, is that on day 4, the sun, moon, and stars *appeared* as distinguishable lights in the sky when the cloud cover that had concealed them dissipated.[66] From a linguistic perspective, C. John Collins says: "The verb *made* in Genesis 1:16 does not specifically mean 'create'; it can refer to that, but it can also refer to 'working on something that is already there' (hence ESV margin), or even 'appointed.'"[67] He argues that this fits with the explanation, given in the very next verse, of the function of the sun and moon as visible lights in the sky. That is, in his view, the verse is speaking about God appointing the role of the sun and moon in the cosmos, and not speaking of either their creation or their appearing.[68]

It is objected that there were no humans around at the time, but does this really count against *appointing* the role of sun and moon in advance of the arrival of humans? Indeed, there is certainly some sense of progression throughout the sequence through which God builds a home suitable for his masterwork, men and women made in his image. In any case, there were surely humans around at the time Genesis was written who would understand this.

However, the exact words used in 1:16 are used again for God "made/created" the land creatures in day 6. Furthermore, the Septuagint version of Genesis uses the identical Greek phrase to say that God "made" the luminaries (1:16) and God "made" the sea creatures (1:21) and God "made" the land animals (1:25). This means that the Jewish scholars who translated the Septuagint thought this was the meaning of the Hebrew words that appear in all three verses. In fact, they are also used in 1:27 for "God made man."

Let us, then, turn to the view that day 4 is speaking of the actual creation of sun, moon, and stars. That could mean the sequence of the days is not chronological or, perhaps, not completely chronological. The main thrust of the text would then be that God is involved in all aspects of creation – which, of course, must be the central message of the passage in any interpretation. In the framework view, day 4 covers exactly the same ground as day 1, but from a different perspective. In day 1 God says: "Let there be light." But then the text goes on to say: "And God separated the light from the darkness. God called the light Day, and the darkness he called Night" (1:4–5). This sounds like the setting up of the solar system. Yet day 1 does not mention the sun or the moon as the reason for the division between day and night. That is added on day 4, where God says, "'Let there be lights in the expanse of the heavens to separate the day from the night . . .' And God made the two great lights" (1:14–16).

Thus, in the framework view, day 4 does not follow day 1 chronologically, but rather revisits day 1, adding details of how day and night were separated by means of sun and moon. Some object that this effectively reduces the number of the days to three instead of six in a rather unnatural way that loses the parallel with the human workweek given in Exodus 20:9–11.

There is a further consideration that might lead us to try *combining* ideas from the different views. We have found that Jewish interpreters by and large interpreted the days as overlaid with metaphorical significance, although they believed in a creation event a finite time ago in the (relatively recent) past. We have looked at Christian interpretations, some of which emphasized chronological order, others logical order – none of them completely satisfying, since day 4 constantly throws a spanner in the works. It is an apparent anomaly, and as a scientist, I am aware that it is sometimes through the study of anomalies that science takes a leap forward. Genesis tells us about familiar things: the heavens and the earth, day and night, and the working week. Then it talks about strange things that do not fit with our experience, like light and vegetation appearing before the sun appears. The order strikes us as rather incongruous, even without taking into account any chronology derived from the fossil record – the incongruity is in Genesis itself.

This has been noted by Jewish polymath Leon Kass, an American physician, scientist, educator, Hebrew scholar, and public intellectual, in his impressive book *The Beginning of Wisdom: Reading Genesis*.[69] Kass tackles the day 4 problem by asking a radical question: "But what if these incongruities should *not* be rationalized away? What if they were *intentionally* arranged incongruously, out of the expected order? What if the text intends, in this way, to challenge, or at least correct, certain aspects of our naïve, untutored perception of our world, a perception that relies mainly on sight and that tacitly holds that seeing is believing?"[70]

Kass points out that the sun is the common feature of all these incongruities. The significance of this in an ancient Near Eastern culture, where the sun was widely worshipped, is obvious. It has often been noted that when the sun is eventually introduced in day 4, it is pointedly not a god but simply a luminary. As Paul Marston points out: "Modern people may find it hard to imagine the shock in Abraham's time of deciding that the moon worshipped in Haran was just a 'lamp.' (If they knew it was just a mirror this would have been even worse!) Imagine the shock of the Egyptians when Ra, the sun god and chief god, turns out also to be a mere lamp created on day 4 for human convenience!"[71]

The text therefore functions as a protest or polemic against idolatry, even though that is not necessarily its primary purpose. However, that is a negative, though important, role and is hardly likely to be the whole story. Kass goes on to develop the ideas of philosopher Leo Strauss, whom I mentioned earlier:

> The striking demotion of the status of the sun leads us to suspect that the author of Genesis is engaged in teaching something besides what came first and what came next, that the sequence of creatures may not be primarily an effort to tell a *historical* or temporal story. Instead, the apparently temporal order could be an image for the ontological order; the temporal sequence

of comings into being could be a vivid literary vehicle for conveying the *intelligible* and *hierarchic* order of the beings that have come to be and *are*. We need a second, and different, look at the biblical sequence.[72]

Kass then draws attention to the parallel between the first three and second three days (the framework view we noted earlier), making the observation that none of the creatures on the first three days can *move*, whereas in the second three days the mobile creatures are arranged in an order of increasing freedom of movement – from the heavenly bodies that are confined to fixed orbits to living things that can move more freely up to humans who can set trajectories for themselves.

He continues: "Having begun to attend not to the temporality but to the logic – or intelligibility – of the sequence, we are in a position to determine the utterly logical and intelligible structure of the entire account. The main principles at work in the creation are *place*, *separation*, *motion*, and *life*, but especially *separation* and *motion*."[73] He points out that the language gives strong support to the idea of separation, with "divide" or "separate" occurring five times explicitly and ten times implicitly in the phrase "after its kind." God divides the light from the darkness; the heavenly lights divide day from night; the firmament or vault of heaven divides the waters above from those below, whereas the creatures without external intervention maintain the distinctiveness of their species by reproducing after their kinds. This is creation/organization by separation, which fittingly proceeds through creation by speech, since the use of words implies the recognition of distinctions.[74] I shall have more to say about this in chapter 5.

I think that the contribution Leon Kass has made is worth thinking about and could easily be missed if our only concern is temporal order rather than logical order. Therefore, an adequate exposition of the text may need to incorporate both aspects. If we do not insist on always prioritizing temporal sequence at the expense of logical sequence, then we can surely recognize temporal aspects – that there was a beginning and that God built up the world to fit it for human habitation by distinct creative acts – but we do not constantly have to look over our shoulders to squeeze a temporal sequence into a scientific mold, nor do we have to squeeze science to fit into a preconceived biblical mold.

Gordon Wenham, in his commentary on Genesis, writes:

> It has been unfortunate that one device which our narrative uses to express the coherence and purposiveness of the creator's work, namely, the distribution of the various creative acts to six days, has been seized on and interpreted over-literalistically, with the result that science and Scripture have been pitted against each other instead of being seen as complementary. Properly understood, Genesis justifies the scientific experience of unity and order in nature. The six-day schema is but one of several means employed in this chapter to stress

the system and order that has been built into creation. Other devices include the use of repeating formulae, the tendency to group words and phrases into tens and sevens, literary techniques such as chiasm and inclusio, the arrangement of creative acts into matching groups, and so on.

Wenham continues: "If these hints were not sufficient to indicate the schematization of the six-day creation story, the very content of the narrative points in the same direction. In particular, evening and morning appear three days before the sun and moon, which are explicitly stated to be for 'days and years' (verse 14). Also, this chapter stands outside the main historical outline of Genesis, each section of which begins, 'This is the (family) history of.'"[75]

We all must face the fact that this is a complex and sophisticated text open to multiple interpretations. I, therefore, reiterate that the fact that Jewish commentators, the early church fathers, and all other serious interpreters have difficulties with the text should give us some comfort and make us humbler. It should also show us that the difficulties are by no means all generated by attempted reconciliations with modern science but arise from attempts to understand the text in its own right. My objective here is to try to make clear what the central message is and to stimulate thought about more peripheral issues. Of course, the reader must make up his or her own mind. It would, however, be sad if failure to come to agreement over the days caused us to miss that central message which we shall consider further in chapter 5.

THE OBJECTION

Finally, I have not forgotten a common objection to what I have been saying in this chapter: that some of the views have been contrived to make Scripture subservient to science, since no one could have arrived at these sophisticated interpretations in the ancient world. Of course, that is perfectly possible. The objection is reasonable, and I take it seriously. At the very least, the second point is clearly justified. Let me respond by saying first that what I have tried to do so far is to look at what the text of Genesis actually says, irrespective of any scientific considerations, and in light of that to consider possible interpretations.

If you say that these seem contrived to fit in with science, I would point out that this is not the first time such a question has arisen. Indeed, I wrote chapter 1 for that very reason. We saw there that the same kind of issue appeared half a millennium ago, not in connection with the age of the earth or the days of Genesis but in connection with the motion of the earth. Copernicus, Rheticus, and Kepler were not claiming that the Bible *taught* the motion of the earth, but that the motion of the earth was consistent with the Bible's teaching. We found that interpreting the foundations and pillars of the earth in terms of the stability of the earth is not a compromise position, but a perfectly reasonable understanding of the text that does not undermine the authority of Scripture, even though this interpretation relies on (new) scientific knowledge.

We need to grasp that this is a perfectly normal way of approaching such matters. We all use it every day. For instance, earlier we discussed the interpretation of the statement "the car is flying down the road" and Jesus' statement "I am the door." What is it that helps us to understand that both statements are to be taken metaphorically and not literally (in the sense of literalistically)? It is our experience of the world. We know about cars, roads, and doors from everyday life. Our response is so instinctive, of course, that we are usually unaware of it. It involves, in essence, a simple reality check: Does our interpretation make sense in the real world? So, regarding science informally as organized knowledge inferred from experience of the world around us, we see that science helps us decide what meaning to go for in both of the examples given.

This enables us to answer the claim that we must interpret the Genesis days as twenty-four-hour days of a single earth week, since that is what most people thought for centuries. If we applied that kind of reasoning to the interpretation of the foundations and pillars of the earth, we would still be insisting that the earth does not move. Yet I have never met anyone, not even a young-earth creationist, who thinks that way. It is just not adequate to choose an interpretation simply on the basis of asking how many people have held it, and for how long.[76] One has to ask why they understood it that way at that time, and whether there are now compelling reasons for changing that understanding. In the case of the motion of the earth, there were strong reasons for changing the interpretation that are now clear and settled. The lesson for us is that we need to be prepared to apply the same kind of thinking to the age of the earth.

The following comment on the moving-earth controversy by two leading young-earth creationists is noteworthy:

> Only when such a position [the classic "unmoved earth" position] became mathematically and observationally "hopeless," should the church have abandoned it. This, in fact, is what the church did.
>
> Young earth creationism, therefore, need not embrace a dogmatic or static biblical hermeneutic. It must be willing to change and admit error. Presently, we can admit that as recent creationists we are defending a very natural biblical account, at the cost of abandoning a very plausible scientific picture of an "old" cosmos. *But over the long term, this is not a tenable position.* In our opinion, old earth creationism combines a less natural textual reading with a much more plausible scientific vision . . . At the moment this would seem the more rational position to adopt.[77]

The major thrust of my argument so far, then, is that I think there are some ways of understanding Genesis 1 that do not compromise the authority and primacy of Scripture and that, at the same time, take into account our increased knowledge of the universe, as Scripture itself suggests we should (Romans 1:19–20).

However, some of my readers will object that I have not mentioned the theological problems associated with believing in an ancient earth, problems that arise not so much in Genesis 1 but in the subsequent chapters. They are quite right. In particular, I have not yet discussed the matter of the entry of death into the world. We must now look at this issue in the context of what Genesis says about the origin of humanity.

NOTES

1. For a historical account, see Ronald L. Numbers, *The Creationists: The Evolution of Scientific Creationism* (1992; repr., Cambridge, MA: Harvard University Press, 2006).

2. Calvin wrote: "Here the error of those is manifestly refuted, who maintain that the world was made in a moment. For it is too violent a cavil to contend that Moses distributes the work which God perfected at once into six days, for the mere purpose of conveying instruction. Let us rather conclude that God himself took the space of six days, for the purpose of accommodating his works to the capacity of men" (*Commentaries on the First Book of Moses Called Genesis* [Grand Rapids: Eerdmans, 1948], 78), https://calvin.edu/centers-institutes/meeter-center/files/john-calvins-works-in-english/Commentary%20001%20-%20Genesis%20Vol.%201.pdf.

3. Rabbi Jonathan Sacks, *The Great Partnership: Science, Religion, and the Search for Meaning* (New York: Schocken, 2012), 351–68.

4. Philo, *On the Creation of the World*, in *The Works of Philo Judaeus*, trans. C. D. Yonge (London: Bell, 1800), 3.

5. Philo, *On the Account of the World's Creation Given by Moses*, in *Philo*, vol. 1, Loeb Classical Library (Cambridge, MA: Harvard University Press, 1981), 15.

6. Philo, *On the Account*, 123.

7. Herman Hailperin, *Rashi and the Christian Scholars* (Pittsburgh, PA: University of Pittsburgh Press, 1963), 44.

8. Maimonides, *Mishneh Torah*, Hilkhot Yesodei ha-Torah 2:2, quoted in Sacks, *Great Partnership*, 352, italics in original.

9. Sacks, *Great Partnership*, 352.

10. Quoted in Sacks, *Great Partnership*, 353.

11. Moses Maimonides, *The Guide for the Perplexed*, 4th rev. ed., trans. M. Friedlaender (New York: Dutton, 1904), book II, chapter XXIX, https://oll.libertyfund.org/title/friedlaender-a-guide-for-the-perplexed#lf0739_head_007.

12. Dov Ginzburg, "The Age of the Earth from Judaic Traditional Literature," *Earth Sciences History* 3, no. 2 (1984): 169–73, www.jstor.org/stable/24135821?seq=1.

13. See Sacks, *Great Partnership*, 356–57.

14. Irenaeus, *Against Heresies*, book 5, in *Ante-Nicene Christian Library: Translations of the Writings of the Fathers*, vol. 9, ed. Alexander Roberts and James Donaldson (Edinburgh: T&T Clark, 1883), 118.

15. Clement of Alexandria, *The Miscellanies*, in *Ante-Nicene Christian Library: Translations of the Writings of the Fathers*, vol. II, ed. Alexander Roberts and James Donaldson (Edinburgh: T&T Clark, 1869), 389.

16. Origen, *On First Principles*, 4.3.1; quoted in Marcus J. Borg, *Reading the Bible Again for the First Time: Taking the Bible Seriously but Not Literally* (San Francisco: HarperSanFrancisco, 2001), 70–71.

17. Origen, *Against Celsus*, in *Ante-Nicene Christian Library: Translations of the Writings of the Fathers*, vol. 10, ed. Alexander Roberts and James Donaldson (Edinburgh: T&T Clark, 1869), 416.

18. Henri de Lubac, *History and Spirit: The Understanding of Scripture according to Origen* (San Francisco: Ignatius, 2007), 159–72.

19. See also Hans Boersma, *Heavenly Participation: The Weaving of a Sacramental Tapestry* (Grand Rapids: Eerdmans, 2011), 146.

20. Basil the Great, *The Nine Homilies of the Hexaemeron and the Letters*, in *Nicene and Post-Nicene Fathers of the Christian Church*, vol. 8, ed. Philip Schaff and Henry Wace (New York: Christian Literature, 1895), 78.

21. Augustine, *The Literal Meaning of Genesis*, in *The Works of Saint Augustine: A Translation for the Twenty-First Century: On Genesis*, vol. 1/13, ed. John E. Rotelle (Hyde Park, NY: New City Press, 2002), 344.

22. Augustine, *The City of God*, ed. G. R. Evans (London: Penguin, 2003), 590–91.

23. Augustine, *The Literal Meaning of Genesis*, vol. 1, in *Ancient Christian Writers: The Works of the Fathers in Translation*, ed. Johannes Quasten, Walter J. Burghardt, and Thomas Comerford Lawler (Mahwah, NJ: Paulist, 1982),148.

24. Augustine, *The City of God*, in *The Works of Aurelius Augustine*, vol. 1, ed. Marcus Dods (Edinburgh: T&T Clark, 1871), 494.

25. C. S. Lewis, *Surprised by Joy: The Shape of My Early Life* (New York: Harcourt, Brace, 1955), 200.

26. *Anagogy* comes from the Greek word *anagoge*, referring to a "climb" or "ascent." It refers to a mystical or spiritual interpretation of Scripture. See the *Oxford English Dictionary*.

27. Boersma, *Heavenly Participation*, 148.

28. Sir Richard Southern, *Robert Grosseteste: The Growth of an English Mind in Medieval Europe*, 2nd ed. (1986; repr., Oxford: Clarendon, 1992), 135.

29. Southern, *Robert Grosseteste*, 209.

30. Southern, *Robert Grosseteste*, 208.

31. For a spectrum of views, see David G. Hagopian, ed., *The Genesis Debate: Three Views on the Days of Creation* (Mission Viejo, CA: Crux, 2001); J. P. Moreland and John Mark Reynolds, eds., *Three Views on Creation and Evolution* (Grand Rapids: Zondervan, 1999).

32. Gordon Wenham, *Genesis 1–15*, Word Biblical Commentary 1 (Waco, TX: Word, 1987), 40.

33. A very useful discussion of this issue appears in C. John Collins, *Genesis 1–4: A Linguistic, Literary, and Theological Commentary* (Phillipsburg, NJ: P&R, 2006), 13ff.

34. In appendix A we discuss some relevant material from the surrounding ancient empires of Egypt, Assyria, and Mesopotamia.

35. For interactive discussions of the main views by well-known representatives, see Hagopian, *Genesis Debate*; Moreland and Reynolds, *Three Views on Creation and Evolution*. There is also a useful account in Roger Forster and Paul Marston, *Reason, Science and Faith* (Crowborough, East Sussex: Monarch, 1999).

36. See J. G. von Herder, *The Spirit of Hebrew Poetry*, trans. James Marsh (Burlington, Ontario: Smith, 1833), 1:58; see also Wenham, *Genesis 1–15*, 6–7; various sources cited in Hagopian, *Genesis Debate*.

37. See David W. Gooding, *According to Luke: A New Exposition of the Third Gospel* (Leicester, UK: Inter-Varsity, 1987), 358–59.

38. John Walton, *The Lost World of Genesis One: Ancient Cosmology and the Origins Debate* (Downers Grove, IL: IVP Academic, 2009), 91.

39. See David Buller, "Creation Is the Temple Where God Rests," *Biologos*, March 6, 2015, https://biologos.org/articles/series/reflections-on-the-lost-world-of-genesis-1-by-john-walton/creation-is-the-temple-where-god-rests; see also Noel K. Weeks, "The Bible and the 'Universal' Ancient World: A Critique of John Walton," *Westminster Theological Journal* 78 (2016): 1–28, http://files1.wts.edu/uploads/images/files/WTJ/WTJ%20Noel%20Weeks%2078.1.pdf.

40. This point has also been made by biblical languages expert Dr. Peter Williams, Warden of Tyndale House, Cambridge University. For a discussion of whether the use of literary symmetry can be consistent with historicity, see Gooding, *According to Luke*, 358–59.

41. Derek Kidner, *Genesis*, Kidner Classic Commentaries (1967; repr., Downers Grove, IL: InterVarsity, 2008), 59.

42. Isaiah 45:18. This is surely a more natural way to read the text than taking it to indicate that the "empty" state of the earth was the result of some great catastrophe, which occurred, so to speak, between verses 1 and 2 of Genesis 1. There is no indication that being "without form and void" is in itself a bad thing. It was simply the starting condition – a bit like a building site.

43. The Hebrew word *bara* is not always used for God's primary causation activity as in Genesis 1:1. Amos 4:13 speaks of God creating the winds, which refers to secondary causation – God creates in this sense through natural processes he has created.

44. We shall come back to the meaning of this statement in chapter 5.

45. This is accepted by both the day-age view and the framework view.

46. See Hebrews 4:3–11.

47. Basil, *Letters and Select Works*, in *Nicene and Post-Nicene Fathers of the Christian Church*, vol. 8, ed. Philip Schaff and Henry Wace (New York: Christian Literature Company, 1895), 64. Basil adds that "if Scripture speaks to us of many ages, saying everywhere 'ages of ages,' we do not see it enumerate them as first, second, and third. It follows that we are hereby shown not so much limits, ends, and successions of ages, as distinctions between various states and modes of action."

48. This, according to scholars, is a possible translation, although Hebrew does not have an equivalent for the English indefinite article *a/an*.

49. A technical word for a section or short passage from a book (from the Greek word meaning "to cut around").

50. Collins, *Genesis 1–4*, 51.

51. *Fiat* is the Latin word for "Let there be," as in "Fiat Lux," which means "Let there be light." On days 3 and 6 there is more than one such expression.

52. Note that this is very different from what is suggested by mainstream evolutionary theory (see appendix D and also my *Cosmic Chemistry: Do God and Science Mix?* [Oxford: Lion Hudson, 2021], chapter 20).

53. See *Cosmic Chemistry*, part 5.

54. I have written about these issues in *Cosmic Chemistry*, chapter 20.

55. A variant of this view is given by Robert Newman and Herman Ecklemann, who suggest that each day opens a new creative period (*Genesis One and the Origin of the Earth* [Leicester, UK: Inter-Varsity Press, 1977], 64–65); see also Newman's chapter "Progressive Creationism," in *Three Views on Creation and Evolution*, ed. J. P. Moreland and John Mark Reynolds (Grand Rapids: Zondervan, 1999), 105–33.

56. See Niles Eldredge and Stephen Jay Gould, "Punctuated Equilibria: An Alternative to Phyletic Gradualism," in *Models in Paleobiology*, ed. Thomas J. M. Schopf (San Francisco: Freeman, Cooper, 1972), 82–115.

57. C. John Collins, *Science and Faith: Friends or Foes?* (Wheaton, IL: Crossway, 2003), 95.

58. That is, unless one thinks, as some do, that the length of the days is itself one of those major doctrines.

59. Quoted in Derek Kidner, *Genesis*, Kidner Classic Commentaries (1967; repr., Downers Grove, IL: InterVarsity, 2008), 59–60.

60. Andrew Parker, *The Genesis Enigma: Why the Bible Is Scientifically Accurate* (New York: Dutton, 2009), xii–xiii, italics in original.

61. Parker, *Genesis Enigma*, 219, italics in original.

62. See Parker, *Genesis Enigma*, 238.

63. Leo Strauss, "Interpretation of Genesis," *Jewish Political Studies Review* 1, no. 1/2 (Spring 1989): 77–92.

64. Richard G. Bower et al., "A Medieval Multiverse?: Mathematical Modelling of the Thirteenth Century Universe of Robert Grosseteste," *Proceedings of the Royal Society A* 470, no. 2167 (July 2014), https://doi.org/10.1098/rspa.2014.0025.

65. See Simon A. Mitton, "Georges Lemaître and the Foundations of Big Bang Cosmology," *The Antiquarian Astronomer* 14 (June 2020): 2–20.

66. Hugh Ross, amongst others, has made this suggestion in *The Genesis Question*, 2nd ed. (Colorado Springs: NavPress, 2001), 43. On this view, the earth started hot (as in the standard "hot big bang" model of physics), and so the sun, even though it had existed from the start, would not have been visible from earth until

the earth had cooled sufficiently to allow the cloud cover to thin and disperse. An observer could have seen the light of the sun but not its source – although it should be pointed out that there were no observers. Also, it is not necessary for the sun to be visible for its light and heat to facilitate the maintenance of life's processes.

67. Collins, *Genesis 1–4*, 57.

68. A point strongly emphasized in John Walton's cosmic temple view.

69. Leon Kass, *The Beginning of Wisdom: Reading Genesis* (Chicago: University of Chicago Press, 2006).

70. Kass, *Beginning of Wisdom*, 30, italics in original.

71. Private communication; used with permission.

72. Kass, *Beginning of Wisdom*, 31, italics in original.

73. Kass, *Beginning of Wisdom*, 32, italics in original.

74. See Kass, *Beginning of Wisdom*, 32–35.

75. Wenham, *Genesis 1–15*, 39–40.

76. Although, of course, it is always important to take note of what people in other times have thought.

77. Paul Nelson and John Mark Reynolds, "Young Earth Creationism," in *Three Views on Creation and Evolution*, ed. Moreland and Reynolds, 73, emphasis added. I am not myself convinced that the old-earth reading is less natural than the young-earth reading, if we are simply thinking in terms of the age of the earth. The reason for this is that, as we saw earlier in this chapter, the text of Genesis 1 separates the initial creation from the first day so that the age of the earth is a logically separate issue from the nature of the days.

CHAPTER 4

HUMAN BEINGS

A Special Creation?

There is probably more controversy today over the origin of human beings than there is over the origin of the universe; and no discussion of creation would be complete without saying something about it. After all, the making of human beings is the pinnacle of God's creation activity, and it has deep significance for our understanding of who and what we and our fellow men and women are. Genesis says that human beings are very special: "So God created man in his own image, in the image of God he created him; male and female he created them" (Genesis 1:27). Jordan Peterson has described this statement as the cornerstone of civilization, which we neglect at our peril.[1]

Jesus himself put the stamp of his divine authority on the creation of humankind. In his discussion with the Pharisees about marriage and divorce, he said, "Have you not read that he who created them from the beginning made them male and female, and said, 'Therefore a man shall leave his father and his mother and hold fast to his wife, and the two shall become one flesh'? So they are no longer two but one flesh. What therefore God has joined together, let not man separate" (Matthew 19:4–6; see also Mark 10:6–9). Jesus draws attention to the fact that these were the very words of the Creator himself: "He who created them . . . *said*."

This is an immensely important reminder of the value, indeed the sacredness, of the marital bond in a world that is increasingly guilty of devaluing it. We men and women desperately need to heed this voice from Genesis in order to avoid the disintegration of our social fabric. For centuries, in the West at least, this biblical teaching has been the foundation of moral values, legislation, and human rights, but it is coming under increasing attack, not only by scientists, but also by leading ethicists building on what scientists have to say. Peter Singer of Princeton University, for example, one of the most influential contemporary ethicists, writes:

> Whatever the future holds, it is likely to prove impossible to restore in full the sanctity-of-life view. The philosophical foundations of this view have been knocked asunder. We can no longer base our ethics on the idea that human beings are a special form of creation made in the image of God, singled out from all other animals, and alone possessing an immortal soul. Our better understanding of our own nature has bridged the gulf that was once thought to lie between ourselves and

other species, so why should we believe that the mere fact that a being is a member of the species *Homo sapiens* endows its life with some unique, almost infinite, value?[2]

In a similar vein, John Gray, emeritus professor of the history of European thought at the London School of Economics, says that over the past two hundred years, philosophy "has not given up Christianity's cardinal error – the belief that humans are radically different from all other animals."[3] The claimed science base for this is, of course, the theory of evolution. Hence the ethical arguments depend not only on the validity and reach of evolutionary theory in biological terms, but also on the validity of philosophical extrapolations and deductions from it.[4]

However, there are influential voices that do not take the view of Singer and Gray, even though they espouse evolutionary theory. Jordan Peterson, for instance, regards the Genesis teaching that human beings – men and women – are made in the image of God as foundational for Western civilization and values. From it he deduces that "each individual has something of transcendent value about them. Man, I tell you, we dispense with that idea at our serious peril."[5]

I wish to comment here on this biblical view. Of all creation, only humans are made in God's image. "The heavens declare the glory of God" (Psalm 19:1), and there is nothing like a night under the magnificent canopy of the stars in a remote part of the country that is free from light pollution to convince one of this (especially if one has a telescope or binoculars). However, we never read in Scripture that the heavens bear the image of God. Only humans do.

Genesis does not deny what chemistry tells us – that all life has a material substrate of common elements. In Genesis 1:11 this fact is implied for vegetation and animals: "Let the earth sprout vegetation"; and also in 1:24: "Let the earth bring forth living creatures." In Genesis 2:7 it is explicitly said of humans: "The LORD God formed the man of dust from the ground and breathed into his nostrils the breath of life, and the man became a living creature." Therefore Genesis affirms that (human) life has a chemical base, but Genesis denies the reductionist addendum of the materialist – that life is nothing but chemistry.

Moreover, in saying that God made man of dust from the ground, Genesis seems to be going out of its way to imply a direct, special creation act rather than suggesting that humans arose, either by natural processes or by God's special activity, out of pre-existing hominids or, indeed, Neolithic farmers.[6]

The New Testament supports this understanding of a special creation of man. Firstly, the genealogy[7] of Jesus given in Luke tracks backwards to "Adam, the son of God" (Luke 3:38). Secondly, Jesus, in his famous discourse on marriage, says, "But from the beginning of creation, 'God made them male and female'" (Mark 10:6). Thirdly, Paul explicitly mentions the making of man from the dust of the ground: "The first man was from the earth, a man of dust; the second man is from heaven" (1 Corinthians 15:47).

We have already noted that the yawning gulf between inorganic and organic matter is underlined in Genesis by the fact that on day 3 God spoke twice. This feature also characterizes day 6, when God also speaks more than once – the first time to say, "Let the earth bring forth living creatures," and the second, "Let us make man."

This surely deliberate repetition is a clear indicator that, as we said earlier, according to Genesis, you cross neither the gulf between nonlife and life nor the gulf between animals and human beings by unguided natural processes. God has to speak his creative word in both instances. Without God speaking there is an unbridgeable discontinuity. The image of God in man was not produced as a result of blind matter fumbling its unguided way through myriad different permutations. Genesis thus challenges atheism's fundamental assertion that human life appeared without the activity of God's mind, so that there is nothing special about human beings.

The difference between animals and humans is further underscored by the fact that God assigned to humans the responsibility of stewardship "over" the animals (Genesis 1:26). Finally, that difference is also the focus in Genesis 2:18–24, where the way in which the narrative is structured shows that the naming of the animals is to be read in the context of finding a helper for Adam. The lesson is that no helper was found fit for (or corresponding to) Adam among the many animal species then existing – therefore, including, be it noted, whatever nonhuman hominids may or may not have existed at the time. It is more than interesting that, according to the Bible, the first lesson Adam was taught was that he was fundamentally different from *all* other creatures.

It has been pointed out that the word for "make" in "let us *make* man in our own image" is from the same root as that used in Psalm 139:15, which reads: "My frame was not hidden from you, when I was being made in secret, intricately woven in the depths of the earth." Clearly, the psalmist was born in the usual way, so why not Adam? But that would mean Adam was not the first man, contrary to what Paul claims. The Genesis account is talking about primary causation, Paul about secondary causation.

However, it is the biblical description of the origin of woman that seems to me to be pivotal. If, as some maintain, it was the case that human females were made from pre-existing hominids, then the Genesis story that the first woman was made from the first man does not fit at all. If it is said to be a metaphor, then I wish to ask: a metaphor for what? Hardly for a divine intervention to turn a hominid into a human. Surely the whole point of the narrative is that no nonhuman animal existed that was suitable as a companion for the man and so no nonhuman animal was used to create one.

Having said that, it would be a rather wooden literalism that insisted on taking from the account the fact that the man named every single species of animal, millions of them in fact, before he was given his companion. That would have taken thousands of years – we are still naming species today! Common sense would say that the point of the account is that Adam gained sufficient knowledge of what animals were and could do to realize that none of them could make a suitable companion for him.

Also, the main thrust[8] of the Genesis account of the creation of woman from man provides little support for the suggestion, made, for instance, by biologist Denis Alexander, not only that there were millions of other humans at that time, but also that Eve was one of them.[9] Alexander does not deny (as many do) the historicity of Adam and Eve. However, it is the nature of his historical understanding that I find difficult to square with the biblical account. His preferred model of events (called model C in his book) is that Adam and Eve were two Neolithic farmers out of all the millions produced by the evolutionary process. God chose these two "to start his new spiritual family on earth, consisting of all who put their trust in God by faith, expressed in obedience to his will."[10]

There is no physical dimension in this understanding of the Genesis creation account: "Just as I can go out on the streets of Cambridge today and have no idea just by looking at people, all of them members of the species *Homo sapiens*, which ones are spiritually alive, so in model C there was no physical way of distinguishing between Adam and Eve and their contemporaries. It is a model about spiritual life and revealed commands and responsibilities, not about genetics."[11]

We read many times in Genesis, as well as in the rest of the Bible, that God chooses to reveal himself spiritually to human beings in a special way – Noah, Abraham, Isaac, and Jacob, for example. However, when Genesis speaks of God revealing himself to human beings, it uses the appropriate language. For instance, "The LORD appeared to Abram."[12] The creation account does not use such language, for Genesis 1 and 2 are not talking about God revealing himself to humans who already existed, but rather revealing to us how those first human beings came to exist in the first place. The text is not describing the calling of existing human beings into fellowship with God, but stating how God physically created human beings from the dust of the earth so that they could have fellowship with him. Moreover, the Genesis narrative makes it evident that Adam and Eve did not need to be called into fellowship with God at the beginning; they were in fellowship with God from the start. It was their sin that broke that fellowship.

Alexander goes on to say, "The text of Genesis 1 makes clear that the whole of humankind without any exception is made in God's image, including certainly all the other millions of people alive in the world in Neolithic times and since."[13] If, however, all human beings who were alive before and at the time of Adam and Eve bore the image of God, then the account of the creation of human beings "in God's image" recorded in Genesis 1 is very different from the story of Adam and Eve in Genesis 2 and indeed must have happened long before it.

What was that event, then, that conferred God's image on the whole of humankind? And what does Alexander mean when he says that Genesis 2 places "the creation of *adam* ... at the beginning of creation"?[14] His interpretation becomes even more difficult to follow when we put the biblical statement "there was *no* man to *work the ground*" (Genesis 2:5, emphasis added) alongside his suggestion that there were millions of Neolithic *farmers* in existence at the time. Did he mean there were hominids that tilled the ground that were not human?

Alexander also says, "Religious beliefs existed before this time, as *people* sought after God or gods in different parts of the world."[15] "People" sounds very like "human," and I presume that Alexander thinks these people were moral beings; otherwise they would not be fully human. If this is the case, it is hard to imagine that there was neither human sin nor human death in the world in the time before God chose to reveal himself to a particular pair. It then becomes difficult to make sense of the biblical teaching that "sin came into the world through one man, and death through sin, and so death spread to all men" (Romans 5:12). How, for example, could the sin of the chosen farmer, Adam, cause the death of those humans who had lived before him? However, this line of thought has entailments that those who hold it might find unwelcome when it comes to the doctrine of salvation.

Furthermore, in one of the curious ironies of evolutionary theory, biologist Alexander argues that human evolution has stopped.[16] Might not the true situation be that it never got started in the first place – that human beings were a direct creation of God?[17]

For the Christian, another consideration bears on this question of the uniqueness of human beings. The central claim of Christianity is that "the Word became flesh and dwelt among us" (John 1:14). God coded himself into humanity. He became a man. There is no question as to this being the central supernatural event in history – a direct action of God of unfathomable significance.

In light of the miracle of the incarnation, I find no difficulty in believing that the human race itself began – indeed, had to begin – with a supernatural intervention. Science cannot rule out that possibility either.[18] What science can tell about human beings, though, is what it can tell us about the universe – namely, that they also had a beginning. What the incarnation tells us is that human beings are unique; they are so created that God himself could and did become one.

THE ANTIQUITY OF HUMANITY

We referred earlier to Archbishop Ussher's calculations regarding the age of the earth. Ussher regarded the days of creation as days of one earth week. Taking the beginning of that week as the creation of the earth, and the end of the week as the starting point for humanity, Ussher used the genealogies given in Genesis to complete his calculation of the age of the earth. His calculation was therefore intimately linked with his estimate of the age of humanity. Our discussion of Genesis up to this point has been concerned with the nature of the days in Genesis 1, and not with questions about the antiquity of humanity.

Regarding calculations made with the use of genealogies, K. A. Kitchen points out, "Within Hebrew and related tradition, such 'official' father-to-son sequences can represent the actual facts of life, or they can be a condensation from an originally longer series of generations."[19] He gives example from Genesis, where lists of sons included grandsons and great-grandsons, and also points out that in the genealogy given in Matthew 1:8, the statement "Jehoram [was] the father of Uzziah" is shorthand for "Jehoram was the father of Ahaziah, who was the father of Joash, who was the father of Amaziah, who was the father of Uzziah." Thus he concludes that in Genesis 1–11, "we see the narratives in some cases presupposing immediate fatherhood . . . But in most cases, one may in principle as easily read the recurring formulae 'A fathered B, and after fathering B lived x years,' as 'A fathered (the line culminating in) B, and after fathering (the line culminating in) B, lived x years.'"[20]

Thus, on the internal evidence of Scripture, the dating of the age of humanity is indeterminate, although whether that indeterminacy is elastic enough to accommodate current paleontological estimates is another matter. There are no easy answers here. I would simply say that the supernatural character of God's creation of humans in his image is much more important than when it happened historically. The same thing is, of course, true of the creation of the universe in the first place.

However, it is important not to confuse things that differ – namely, the age of the universe, the age of the earth, the age of life, and the age of humanity. Clearly, the earth is younger than the universe; biological life is younger than the earth; and human life is younger than biological life.

A THEOLOGICAL OBJECTION: DEATH BEFORE ADAM'S SIN?

The idea that the earth may have existed long before the creation of human beings creates a theological problem – the existence of death before the entry of sin into the world. This matter arises because of the statement of the apostle Paul: "Therefore, just as sin came into the world through one man, and death through sin, and so death spread to all men because all sinned" (Romans 5:12). The argument is simply that since death is a consequence of human sin, no death could have occurred before man sinned. This is clearly a serious issue with profound implications for the doctrine of salvation, since, as has often been pointed out, if Paul is wrong in his diagnosis of the origin of sin and death, how can we expect him to be right regarding its solution?

I am now faced with an additional problem. In a short, introductory book, as this is intended to be, that concentrates mainly on the time of creation, it is simply impossible to include a detailed discussion of the nature and provenance of the events described in Genesis 3, important though they are. So I shall have to content myself (and thus risk discontenting some readers!) with sketching some of the ideas that seem to me to bear directly on the question as stated above.

The Genesis account of the entry of sin into the world (Genesis 3:1–7) is one of the most fascinating parts of the Bible. The action takes place in the Garden of Eden and has to do with its plants, animals, and humans or, more accurately, with a special tree, the tree of the knowledge of good and evil; a special animal, the serpent; and, of course, Adam and Eve.

The first humans have been placed in the garden and told that they may eat of every tree (including, by implication, that other special tree, the tree of life) except for the tree of the knowledge of good and evil. They are warned that if they eat the fruit of this tree, they will die. That is, they have the capacity to eat of all of the trees without exception, but not the permission to eat the fruit of one particular tree. Here we have the basic ingredients that define human beings as moral beings. God has given them the ability to say yes to him by not eating the fruit of the prohibited tree, and to say no to him by eating its fruit.

We need not discuss what the nature of the fruit of the tree was, or wonder what quality it must have had so that eating of it should produce the knowledge of good and evil. To interpret it that way is to miss the point of the story. To eat from any tree, indeed, to do anything at all, from whatever motive, that is contrary to the will and word of our Creator and the Ruler of this world is itself lawlessness. It is a frame of mind that asserts the creature's will against the Creator's, that pushes the Creator aside and makes central to everything the pursuit of one's own egotistical interests and interpretation of life. That is, in principle, what "sin" is. The second-century writer Theophilus of Antioch (AD 115–181) said: "It was not the tree, as some think, but the disobedience which had the death in it."[21]

We are next introduced to one of the chief actors in the drama – the serpent. We are told that it "was more crafty than any other beast of the field that the LORD God had made" (Genesis 3:1). It turns out to be very different from the other creatures: it is clever, and it can speak. It engages Eve in a conversation about the significance of eating the fruit of the prohibited tree of the knowledge of good and evil. We need to pause and think about a question many readers may now be asking: Who or what was this serpent whose insinuations triggered such a seismic catastrophe from which the world has been reeling ever since? It appears unannounced on the page of Genesis, simply described as one of the creatures God had made. But that is already telling us something, and simultaneously raising many questions. For this serpent is a creature, so God is ultimately responsible for its existence. Yet it is clearly opposed to God. In other words, Genesis is saying there was already an alien enemy in the earth, a being that, apparently, had the capacity to disobey God, had actually done so, and was now encouraging the first humans to follow suit.

Now some people dismiss all of this as primitive mythology. Yet others think it is mythology but far from primitive in that it communicates a powerful message. One of them is Jordan Peterson, who, in the words of Ron Dart's introduction to the book he edited, *Myth and Meaning in Jordan Peterson*, "takes biblical stories in a mythical sense, not getting hung up on the historicity of them, and will ask almost what a spiritual director would ask: 'What does this story mean for you on your journey?' All of a sudden, people realize that the text can speak to them."[22] Peterson's famous expositions of Genesis, which have received millions of views on YouTube, have that effect – "the genius of the Bible is that it transcends time and history and speaks to the human soul," as Dart says.[23]

But do you really have to leave time and history behind and affirm a mythological interpretation in order for the Bible to speak to your soul? I, for one, do not think so. Of course, we must present the text as one that speaks to the human soul today. It must be seen to say something that has real impact. One has to admit with sadness that it is sometimes the case that those who, like me, do not take a mythological approach to Genesis and have a high view of Scripture fail to see and extract enough meaning in the text for it to have any real impact at all. I find this a challenge to myself.

Getting back to the matter at hand, it is ironic that some people who reject the Genesis account of the fall as having nothing to do with reality are prepared to accept without question the verdict of scientists who inform them that the universe must be teeming with extraterrestrial life, even though they have not as yet discovered evidence of its existence. The Bible claims that humans are not the only beings in the universe – there are angels, and there are evil demonic powers. Could it be that God's great enemy Satan, the Accuser, is using an animal to attack God through human beings?

The New Testament is not embarrassed to tell us that the Lord Jesus himself was opposed not only by human malevolence but by a nonhuman, supernatural being, the devil, who is called Satan, the Accuser. Now Genesis 3 does not use any of these words, but it is not hard to see from subsequent Scripture that behind the serpent described in that chapter there is the malevolent figure of the devil – "that ancient serpent," as he is called in the last book of the Bible (Revelation 12:9; 20:2).

The key thing therefore about the serpent is not so much what species it belonged to but the fact that it represents Satan. Does that mean a literal animal could not have been involved? Or was it Satan taking on the form of an animal? Opinions differ on this, but several things are worth saying. Firstly, on one occasion God used a literal donkey and spoke through it to rebuke the prophet Balaam. So it is not beyond the bounds of reason that the enemy could have used a snake to mount an attack on the first humans. Secondly, Jesus tells the following parable about demon-possession in Matthew 12:43–45:

"When the unclean spirit has gone out of a person, it passes through waterless places seeking rest, but finds none. Then it says, 'I will return to my house from which I came.' And when it comes, it finds the house empty, swept, and put in order. Then it goes and brings with it seven other spirits more evil than itself, and they enter and dwell there, and the last state of that person is worse than the first. So also will it be with this evil generation."

Also, there is the description of Judas by Jesus himself: "One of you is a devil" (John 6:70). Later on, John says of Judas: "Then after he had taken the morsel, Satan entered into him" (John 13:27). It would seem that Satan can, in some sense, enter into a human. Jude 6 might be speaking of something similar. We must admit that reality is more complex than we think or imagine, and no matter what interpretation we adopt, the important thing, of course, is that it is a real being, Satan, who does the tempting. In the temptations of Jesus there is no mention of a snake. There was only the devil. Effectively, the serpent is Satan.

The serpent first subtly questions the prohibition: "Did God actually say, 'You shall not eat of any tree in the garden'?" (Genesis 3:1). Eve answers, rather inaccurately, by saying that God has forbidden even touching the tree, let alone eating of it. The serpent then responds with outright denial: "You will not surely die." To this it adds, "God knows that when you eat of it your eyes will be opened, and you will be like God, knowing good and evil" (3:4–5).

The serpent contrives, by a devious manipulation of half-truth and appeal to her interest in food, her aesthetic sense, and her desire for insight and fulfilment – all originally God-given – to drive a wedge between her and her Creator. The snake's power of persuasion is such that Eve rejects the word of God, takes the forbidden fruit,[24] and offers it to Adam, and they both eat.

In that searing moment they discover that the enlightenment they receive is far from what they expected. Knowledge of good and evil obtained in this way is not the kind of knowledge one wants. For instead of finding life, they begin to experience death, as God had said they would. They do not at once die in the physical sense. That effect of their action will inevitably ensue in due course. Human life, as we learn from Genesis 2, has many aspects; its lowest level is physical life, to which we must add those other things that make life life – aesthetics, food, work, human relationships, and a moral relationship with God.

Human death, then, will involve the unweaving of all of this. It will first mean the death of fellowship with God, and the first result of this death is a pathetic attempt to hide from God in the garden. The deadly rupture of fellowship with God will then lead inexorably to all the other levels of death – aesthetic death, death of human relationships, and so on, until we reach the lowest level of death, which turns our bodies back to molecules of dust.

In Genesis 3 God pronounces a judgement on the serpent for what it did. Part of this judgement is: "I will put enmity between you and the woman, and between your offspring and her offspring; he shall bruise your head, and you shall bruise his heel" (3:15). We note that the serpent is to have offspring that will be opposed to the offspring of the woman. The offspring are not literal snakes, however. Jesus tells us who they are. He once said to bigoted religious people who were accusing him: "You are of your father the devil" (John 8:44). The offspring of the serpent were human beings who adopt Satan's hatred of God.

But one particular offspring of the woman, that is, an actual human being, will triumph over the serpent by bruising his head. The rest of Genesis will be the first part of the story of the offspring (or seed) of the woman – the seed of Abraham, Isaac, and Jacob – a story that will reach its climax in the Offspring, or Seed, Jesus Christ. That is, the promise here is not simply that God will triumph – that was never in doubt. It is that humanity will triumph in Jesus Christ.

Now, however intriguing all of this may be, we cannot divert into further discussion of it. I simply wish to make the point that, according to Scripture, evil in the universe appears to antedate the sin of Adam and Eve. C. S. Lewis put it this way:

> Now it is impossible at this point not to remember a certain sacred story which, though never included in the creeds, has been widely believed in the Church and seems to be implied in several Dominical, Pauline, and Johannine utterances – I mean the story that man was

not the first creature to rebel against the Creator, but that some older and mightier being long since became apostate and is now the emperor of darkness and (significantly) the Lord of this world.[25]

Lewis goes on to say, "It seems to me, therefore, a reasonable supposition, that some mighty created power had already been at work for ill on the material universe, or the solar system, or, at least, the planet Earth, before ever man came on the scene: and that when man fell, someone had, indeed, tempted him . . . If there is such a power, as I myself believe, it may well have corrupted the animal creation before man appeared."[26]

Whatever the meaning of the details, the timeless implications are clear – disaster occurred through rejection of the word of God. In his contribution to *Myth and Meaning in Jordan Peterson*, Bruce Riley Ashford references the work of Francis George Steiner, a French-American literary critic, essayist, philosopher, and novelist: "In *Grammars of Creation*, Steiner turns his attention to God as the Author of creation, arguing that we must reject the late modern rejection of God's creative word. [Quoting Steiner,] 'I believe this dislocation, this tidal wave against the word, to be more severe and consequential than any other in modernity.' Without God's creative word, there is nothing to fund and shape human creativity."[27]

With this all too brief sketch we turn to look more closely at what the apostle Paul says about the entry of sin into the world – and what he does not say. He says that death spread to *all human beings* as a result of Adam's sin; he does not say that death spread to *all living things* (Romans 5:12). That is, what Scripture actually says is that *human* death is a consequence of sin.[28] That makes sense. Humans are moral beings, and human death is the ultimate wages of moral transgression. We do not think of plants and animals in terms of moral categories. We do not accuse the lion of sinning when it kills an antelope or even a human being. Paul's deliberate and careful statement would appear to leave open the question of death at levels other than human.

Indeed, since fruit and vegetables[29] are explicitly mentioned as the human (God-given) diet in Genesis, plant life can scarcely be an issue here. Plant death cannot therefore have been a consequence of the first human sin, even though plant death is death. It is part of the cycle of nature on which all life depends. What about the animals? Whales, for instance, are mammals, and they do not live on green vegetation. Their food is living seafood; and so, by eating, whales cause death. The same is true of many sea and land creatures. Did they have some alternative source of food before Adam sinned? Hardly.

In a similar way, the view that animal death did not exist before humans sinned would make the existence of predators problematic. The woodpecker has astonishingly powerful muscles in its neck to enable it to peck out insects. Some snakes secrete poisons, and some fish can launch bolts of electricity that stun their prey. Furthermore, many animals and fish have camouflage systems to avoid predation. There are insects that *look* poisonous to birds, even though they aren't actually poisonous. If there was no death of any kind before the first human sin (and therefore no predation), did these exquisitely complex neck muscles, poison sacs, electrical organs, and camouflage systems come into existence as a result of that sin? If that is so, would it not make that sin the trigger of an extensive creation process – a feature that seems very unlikely, and one on which the Bible is silent? Or did God foresee the change, build the mechanisms into the creatures in advance, and then do something to set them in operation?

I begin to think that Occam's razor[30] may need to be applied at this point in order to restrict the multiplication of unnecessary hypotheses – that is, if the theological problem arises from going beyond what Paul actually says.

Now, the question will at once arise as to what Paul then means by his later statement: "For the creation was subjected to futility, not willingly, but because of him who subjected it, in hope that the creation itself will be set free from its bondage to corruption and obtain the freedom of the glory of the children of God" (Romans 8:20–21). Surely it will be said that this must mean, must it not, that all death is a result of human sin?

Once more we need to observe exactly what is being said. Paul speaks of decay and corruption. Think of what happens to flowers. Daffodils can get disease. However, daffodils, whether diseased or not, die down in the early summer.

Only the bulbs are left, which then grow again the following year. Is that process of dying down the same thing as disease? Surely not. This is part of the cycle of nature. Is it a good thing, part of the original creation, or is it a result of sin? Similarly, salmon can become diseased. But that is not the same thing as salmon dying after they have spawned. Once more, this strange phenomenon is part of the cycle of nature. Again, is this a good thing, or is it a result of sin?

Is it therefore possible that corruption, disease, and human death may well be a consequence of sin, but that plant and animal death, as part of the cycle of nature, are not?[31] One might then reasonably argue that Romans 8:20–21 is carefully written to refer to decay and corruption as distinct from death. Once more the key is to observe exactly what Scripture says.

It is also helpful to think about the circumstances in which human death was introduced into the world. We are told that there was a tree of life in the garden to which free access was granted (Genesis 2:16). One consequence of Adam's sin was that access to that tree was barred, "'lest he reach out his hand and take also of the tree of life and eat, and live forever' – therefore the LORD God sent him out from the garden of Eden" (3:22–23). This could mean, as many think, that Adam had never eaten the fruit of that tree, and God was grateful he hadn't. But could it also mean that this special food was near him while he was in the garden, so that all he needed to do was put forth his hand to take it? Once he was outside the garden, he could no longer do that, since the tree was only in one place – namely, the middle of the garden.[32]

This leads to the question: At creation, did human beings have essential, inherent immortality that was removed when they sinned? Or, in light of the New Testament's explicit statement, "[God] alone has immortality" (1 Timothy 6:16), does it follow that Adam never had intrinsic immortality but was dependent from the beginning on regular access to an external source of food (the tree of life) for continued existence?

The relevance of this to the question of nonhuman death is simply this: What was the status of other living creatures, for example, animals and birds, with respect to the tree of life? Did they have intrinsic immortality, or did they not? If they did (which might be somewhat surprising if humans didn't), what did God subsequently do to remove that immortality, as distinct from what he did to man? There is no mention of removing birds and animals from the garden. And yet, if the animals and birds were also dependent on the tree of life, what about those animals and birds that were presumably outside the garden from the beginning? From the biblical text one does not get the impression that the entire world was like Eden. Indeed, the very opposite seems to be implied by the statement that God planted a garden. That raises even more questions: What was the difference, exactly, between the inside and the outside of that garden? When we think of gardens, we tend to think only of the plants, but in the account of the Garden of Eden, there is clear interest in the animals as well as the plants. What, then, was the situation of not only the flora but the fauna outside the idyllic Garden of Eden? We can only speculate.

Whatever the answers are to these questions, it would seem that Scripture itself leaves open the possibility that animals died before sin entered the world without affecting the fact that human death was a consequence of that sin.[33] This should not be taken to mean, however, that I think I have solved all the questions that arise here. In particular, two things spring at once to mind. The first is that, where does animal *pain* fit into all of this? For, it will be said, if predation is part of the cycle of nature, how can that be a good thing when, as we are increasingly aware, it seems frequently to be attended by the most horrific suffering on the part of the victims – at least in so far as we can understand animal suffering? Was there, for instance, a difference between the behavior of animals outside the Garden of Eden and that of those in the idyllic situation inside? If so, what was the cause?

One thing at least seems to be implied by the Genesis 3 account of the fall as discussed above: that a dark power had corrupted at least part of the animal creation. Could it be that this is the direction in which we must look in order to begin to comprehend the origin of the pain and suffering that seem to permeate the animal kingdom?

The question of the origin of humans – are we made in the image of God, or are we cast out into the sea of the possible random permutations of matter without any ultimate significance? – is of major importance for our concept of our human identity; and it is therefore not surprising that ferocious efforts are being made to minimize the difference between humans and animals, on the one hand, and the difference between humans and machines, on the other. Such efforts are driven, at least in part, by the secular conviction that naturalism must in the end triumph over theism by its reductionist arguments in removing the last vestige of God from his creation. Human beings must in the end turn out to be nothing but physics and chemistry.

It is important, therefore, to combat such atheist physicalism by presenting biblical theism as a credible alternative that, far from leading to intellectual suicide, makes sense of the data, whereas atheistic reductionism does not.

THE WAY FORWARD

We have seen how the change from a fixed-earth to a moving-earth interpretation of Scripture came about as a result of gradually increasing scientific evidence that the earth is in motion. The parallel evidence regarding the antiquity of the universe is more recent, coming to us first from the disciplines of geology and most recently from advances in astronomy and cosmology. Of course, I am well aware that the biological theory of evolution demands an ancient earth, and for many people this is a major factor in their thinking. However, the cosmological evidence is completely independent of biology, and it is therefore perfectly possible to accept that evidence without committing oneself to thinking that life has arisen by an unguided materialistic evolutionary process. It is simply false to suggest, as some do, that the only alternative to young-earth creationism is to accept the Darwinian model.

I discuss this and other related issues in my book *Cosmic Chemistry*.[34] I also discuss the implications of the fact that the neo-Darwinian modern synthesis is proving inadequate in the view of an increasing number of leading biologists. I have also devoted appendix D in this book to the question of theistic evolution (= evolutionary creationism, or evotheism).

Now, all true scientists are aware, of course, that science is not infallible. Theories change (for example, as we have seen regarding the motion of the earth). Many scientists, though, are critical realists. They believe they are making steps towards grasping the truth about the universe, but they are prepared to modify their theories if the evidence warrants it. We Christians need to remind ourselves of the two dangers outlined at the end of chapter 2. Firstly, we must beware of tying our exposition of Scripture so closely to science that the former falls if the latter changes. Secondly, we would be very unwise to ignore science through obscurantism or fear, and thus present to the world an image of a Christianity that is anti-intellectual. No Christian has anything to fear from true science. Many Christians have made, and continue to make, first-rate contributions to science.

So what is the best way forward? There seem to me to be four salient considerations:

1. The current scientific evidence for an ancient earth.
2. The honest and admirable admission of prominent young-earth creationists that "recent creationists should humbly agree that their view is, at the moment, implausible on purely scientific grounds. They can make common cause with those who reject naturalism, like old earth creationists, to establish their most basic beliefs."[35]
3. The fact that Genesis, though it could be interpreted in terms of a young earth, does not require such an interpretation. There are other possible interpretations in terms of an ancient earth that do not compromise the authority of Scripture.
4. The fact that we do not know everything. Humility is often seen in the greatest scientists. It is also a foundational Christian virtue.

Considerations essentially the same as the first three of these, with "young-earth" replaced by "fixed-earth," would have weighed increasingly with people in the years after Copernicus and Galileo and would have made them more and more confident in affirming the new interpretation that fitted more closely with the increased understanding of the universe. There is no reason this cannot happen today. Just as it was no shame or compromise in the past for people to change their minds over the motion of the earth, so it is no shame or compromise today for people to change their minds about the age of the earth. After all, it was only recently that scientists were persuaded that there was a beginning! That spurs us to recall the fourth factor listed above – the need for humility.

A NECESSARY POSTSCRIPT

I do not wish to leave the matter just here. If I do, readers may think the only reason for looking at Genesis 1 is to try to settle the matter of its relationship to science. That would be a pity, because it has many other important things to say, as we shall now explain in our final chapter.

NOTES

1. See Jordan Peterson, "Biblical Series II: Genesis 1: Chaos and Order Transcript," www.jordanbpeterson.com/transcripts/biblical-series-ii.

2. Peter Singer, "Sanctity of Life or Quality of Life?" *Pediatrics* 72, no.1 (July 1983): 128–29, http://digitalcollections.library.cmu.edu/awweb/awarchive?type=file&item=594077.

3. John Gray, *Straw Dogs* (London: Granta, 2003), 37.

4. For more on these matters, I refer the reader once more to my book *Cosmic Chemistry: Do God and Science Mix?* (Oxford: Lion Hudson, 2021), part 4.

5. Peterson, "Chaos and Order Transcript."

6. See the next section below.

7. For comments on genealogies in the Bible and the antiquity of humans, see below.

8. As distinct from the detail of what precisely was involved in the creation of woman, but note that Paul explicitly says that "Adam was formed first, then Eve" (1 Timothy 2:13), and "woman [was made] from man" (1 Corinthians 11:8).

9. See Denis Alexander, *Creation or Evolution: Do We Have to Choose?* (Oxford: Monarch, 2014), 236–39.

10. Alexander, *Creation or Evolution*, 237.

11. Alexander, *Creation or Evolution*, 237–38.

12. Genesis 17:1; 18:1.

13. Alexander, *Creation or Evolution*, 238.

14. Alexander, *Creation or Evolution*, 193.

15. Alexander, *Creation or Evolution*, 237, emphasis added.

16. See, for example, Alexander, *Creation or Evolution*, 232.

17. In connection with the obvious fact that there are variations in human beings, it is noteworthy that Paul informs the philosophers at Athens that God made all nations from one man (Acts 17:26).

18. Science cannot rule out this kind of miracle, despite the attempts by thinkers from David Hume to the New Atheists to convince us to the contrary; see Lennox, *Cosmic Chemistry*, chapter 6.

19. K. A. Kitchen, *On the Reliability of the Old Testament* (Grand Rapids: Eerdmans, 2003), 440.

20. Kitchen, *On the Reliability*, 441.

21. *Theophilus to Autolucus* 13, in *Ante-Nicene Christian Library Translations of the Writings of the Fathers*, vol. 3, ed. Alexander Roberts and James Donaldson (Edinburgh: T&T Clark, 1869), 90.

22. Ron Dart, ed., *Myth and Meaning in Jordan Peterson: A Christian Perspective* (Bellingham, WA: Lexham, 2020), 3.

23. Dart, *Myth and Meaning*, 3.

24. Nowhere is an apple mentioned.

25. C. S. Lewis, *The Problem of Pain* (1940; repr., New York: Macmillan, 1962), 133–34.

26. Lewis, *Problem of Pain*, 134–35.

27. Bruce Riley Ashford, "Jordan Peterson and the Chaos of Our Secular Age," in Dart, *Myth and Meaning in Jordan Peterson*, 12.

28. See John Walton, *The Lost World of Genesis One* (Downers Grove, IL: InterVarsity, 2009), 100.

29. Derek Kidner points out that the assigning of plants for food (Genesis 1:29–30) to all creatures "must not be pressed to mean that all were once herbivorous, any more than to mean that all plants were equally edible to all. It is a generalization that, directly or indirectly, all life depends on vegetation, and the concern of the verse is to show that all are fed from God's hand" (*Genesis*, Kidner Classic Commentaries [1967; repr., Downers Grove, IL: InterVarsity, 2008], 57).

30. Attributed to the fourteenth-century English Franciscan thinker William of Ockham, this is the general principle that one should favour a hypothesis

that makes the fewest new assumptions among competing hypotheses that are equal in other respects. It does not (falsely) assert that the simplest explanation is always likely to be the correct one.

31. We might add to that a detail concerning the animal sacrifices that were used in Old Testament times to teach Israel the connection between sin and death, and thereby to point forward to the death of Christ as a sacrifice for sin. In the instructions for how to perform the sacrifices, it is strongly emphasized that the sacrificial animals should not be diseased. Disease was, in that sense, to be distinguished from death (see Leviticus 1:3, 10; 3:1, 6; and many other references).

32. There are endless arguments about how we are to understand the tree – literally or metaphorically. In light of our earlier discussion, if we take the tree as metaphorical, we shall immediately be asked the question – a metaphor for what reality? Could it just be that the ancient legends about an elixir of life have a factual basis – that there once was an actual tree of life? In any case we are not (contrary to popular thought) told what the fruit was, so that the important thing is what was represented by it.

33. It is interesting to note that the instruction about vegetation as food for animals (Genesis 1:30) was given to the humans and not to the animals. Why? One possibility might be as follows. The humans had just been told what their food was to be. They had been commanded to subdue the fish, animals, and birds. It would be important for them to know that the subduing did not include keeping the animals away from the humans' food, suggesting that at least some of them may have had nonvegetarian food. In Genesis 9 there is no explicit commandment to the animals to be carnivorous from now on. But humans are allowed from then on to kill and eat animals.

34. See Lennox, *Cosmic Chemistry*, parts 4–5.

35. Paul Nelson and John Mark Reynolds, "Young Earth Creationism," in *Three Views on Creation and Evolution*, ed. J. P. Moreland and John Mark Reynolds (Grand Rapids: Zondervan, 1999), 51.

CHAPTER 5

THE MESSAGE OF GENESIS 1

The book of Genesis is foundational for the rest of the Bible. Its opening chapter does something of incalculable importance: it lays down the basis of a biblical worldview.[1] It gives to us humans a metanarrative, a big story into which our lives can be fitted and from which they can derive meaning, purpose, and value. This chapter is devoted to that big story.

GOD EXISTS

One of the most basic big questions we can ask is, what is the nature of ultimate reality? The central tenet of the biblical worldview is that the ultimate reality is God: "In the beginning, God . . ." Genesis is here making a profound truth claim: that there is a God. The claim is first stated without any supporting evidence – a circumstance that should not mislead us into imagining that the author of Genesis had no evidence. Both Genesis and the rest of the Bible will subsequently offer that evidence. However, the very manner in which Genesis begins reminds us that every worldview must start somewhere. The biblical worldview begins with God; the atheist worldview begins with the universe or, indeed, nothing.

However, Genesis 1 does not only tell us that there is a God; it tells us a great deal about him.

GOD IS THE ETERNAL CREATOR

"In the beginning, God created the heavens and the earth." Genesis 1:1 thus majestically announces the fact of creation. This is not only a truth claim about God; it is a truth claim about the physical universe. Although the text does not explicitly say that the universe was created from nothing (sometimes expressed by the Latin phrase *ex nihilo*), there are strong arguments for understanding it this way, as many scholars do.

Firstly, the phrase "the heavens and the earth" is most likely to be a merism[2] denoting "everything in the material universe," in which case the implication of Genesis 1:1 is ex nihilo creation. Secondly, in possibly the clearest New Testament statement of all on the topic, Revelation 4:11 reads: "Worthy are you, our Lord and God, to receive glory and honor and power, for you created all things, and by your will they existed and were created." The implication is that the universe came to exist because God created it at some point, so we may deduce that it was created from nothing, since there was nothing in existence from which to create it – however hard it is for us to get our minds around the idea. All of these later statements have clear roots in Genesis 1:1.

The assertion that God created the physical universe is of paramount importance. It answers the question: Why is there something rather than nothing? It implies that this universe cannot explain itself, as secular atheism by definition must maintain. It tells us that this material universe is not the ultimate reality; God is.

It is important, of course, not to confuse the fact of creation with the manner or the timing of creation. I mention this because it sometimes happens that failure to sort out problems connected with the manner and timing of creation stops people from believing in the fact that creation occurred. An illustration from science can help us grasp the issue here. Stephen Hawking says that space-time began in a singularity, where the laws of physics break down.[3] The moment of creation, therefore, poses an immense problem for science. But this does not stop most scientists from believing the fact that there was a beginning. The important thing for these scientists is that there is scientific evidence for a beginning, even though science cannot comprehend the nature of that beginning.[4] We should bear this attitude in mind when we come to Genesis.

Genesis 1:1 anticipates the fuller revelation given to us by John at the beginning of his gospel: "In the beginning was the

Word, and the Word was with God, and the Word was God. He was in the beginning with God. All things were made through him, and without him was not any thing made that was made" (John 1:1–3). The word translated "made" means "came to be." God is eternal and uncreated. He did not come to be; he always was. The universe, on the other hand, did "come to be." It was not always there – another strong confirmation, by the way, of ex nihilo creation.

The Genesis account, though not written as a polemic, is therefore diametrically opposed to all idolatrous interpretations of the universe, whether of the ancient pagan kind or the modern secular variety. Genesis clashes head-on with the Babylonian, Canaanite, and Egyptian polytheisms, just as much as the gospel of John contradicts their Greek and Roman equivalents. In particular, ancient Near Eastern accounts typically contain theogonies,[5] which describe how the gods are generated from primeval matter. These gods are, therefore, mere deifications of nature and its powers. This means that such ancient worldviews stand much closer to contemporary materialism than it might first appear. There are contemporary physicists, like Paul Davies, for example, who argue that the fine-tuning of the universe indicates that there is great intelligence somewhere. But they hold nevertheless that this intelligence must have evolved from primitive matter; it is, in that sense, of material origin. Genesis and the gospel of John negate the materialistic/naturalistic paradigm in which everything starts with mass/energy, a quantum vacuum, or even nothing.[6]

One of Richard Dawkins's main *God Delusion* arguments is that if God created everything, we would have to ask who created God. Quite frankly, it is a foolish argument that demonstrates ignorance of elementary philosophical reasoning. For the very asking of this question reveals at once that Dawkins has in mind a *created* God: "Who *created* God?"

Created gods certainly are a delusion. However, the God who is revealed in Genesis is uncreated, so that the "who created God argument" falls to the ground. Dawkins's difficulty must be that he cannot believe in something eternal. Why not? Science certainly does not tell us there is nothing eternal. In fact, the notion of an eternal universe or eternal energy has dominated human thought for centuries and still has not disappeared from academic circles. Furthermore, if Dawkins's question is valid, it can be turned back on him. He believes that the universe created him. Therefore, we are justified in asking him: Who created your creator?

The point here is that *all* such questionings must stop with what the questioner believes to be ultimate reality. As we have seen, for the atheist, the ultimate reality is the universe, and for the theist, the ultimate reality is God. Genesis tells us that God is primary, and the universe derivative. This worldview is the exact opposite of ancient polytheism and contemporary secularism, both of which assume that matter is primary and everything else, including mind, is derivative.

GOD IS DISTINCT FROM HIS CREATION

Furthermore, according to Genesis, God created the universe, but he is not identical with it. Noticeably, the sun, moon, and stars are described purely physically, as "lights." There is no hint of conferring any kind of divinity on them, as in the contemporary pagan mythologies. Nor is the universe some kind of emanation out of God, like sunrays emanate from the sun. Matter is made out of nothing, not out of God. The Genesis account, therefore, bears no traces of pantheism.

Nor is God the remote, deistic "god of the scientists," who started the universe and then retired from the scene, taking no further interest in it. Indeed, the main bulk of the Genesis narrative is devoted to relationships between human beings and God – and, of course, relationships among human beings themselves.

The very fact that such relationships are possible has to do with another profound characteristic of God revealed in Genesis 1.

GOD IS PERSONAL

The phrases "God said," "God saw that it was good," "God blessed," and, above all, "God created man in his own image . . . male and female he created them" are clear indications that God is a person and not a force. There are dangers in a Star Wars mentality that conceives of God as "the

Force," for we are persons and therefore assume, correctly, that we are superior to forces. We harness and use forces, so if we conceive of God as a force, we might wrongly imagine that God is some power we can harness and use rather than regarding him as our Creator and Lord who is worthy of and due our allegiance and worship. It is for him to use us, not for us to use him.

GOD IS A FELLOWSHIP

Genesis 1 talks about the Spirit of God "hovering over the face of the waters" (verse 2) and records God as saying: "Let *us* make man in *our* image" (Genesis 1:26, emphasis added). No explanation is given at this point, but these statements surely anticipate New Testament teaching on the Trinity.[7] This impression is heightened by the repeated use of the phrase "And God said . . ." Creation involves the word of God. Concentrating on that fact, the apostle John begins his gospel with the magnificent statement "In the beginning was the Word, and the Word was with God, and the Word was God. He was in the beginning with God. All things were made through him" (John 1:1–3).

John swiftly identifies the Word with Jesus Christ: "The Word became flesh and dwelt among us, and we have seen his glory, glory as of the only Son from the Father, full of grace and truth" (John 1:14). Thus, God is revealed to us as a tri-unity, a fellowship of Father, Son, and Holy Spirit.

The apostle Paul says of Christ, "He is the image of the

invisible God, the firstborn of all creation. For by him all things were created, in heaven and on earth, visible and invisible, whether thrones or dominions or rulers or authorities – all things were created through him and for him. And he is before all things, and in him all things hold together" (Colossians 1:15–17).

These are staggering claims to make about anyone in any age, let alone in the twenty-first century. They clearly imply that Christ created space-time. It was he who conceived and, with unimaginable energy and power, spoke into being a material universe, governed by intricate laws that he himself designed. It was his mind that was the mind of God that thought into existence the blueprint for matter, life, and consciousness. Nothing makes sense about Jesus Christ unless he is precisely who he claimed to be – the Word of God incarnate. Science, as has often been said, cannot rule God out. Jesus Christ has ruled him in.

GOD HAS A GOAL IN CREATION

We noted earlier that the primary impression given by the biblical creation account is that God did not do everything at once. This striking fact immediately raises in our minds the question: What is the goal of the sequence of days? What are they leading up to? The narrative starts with, "In the beginning, God created the heavens and the earth." Then we are told that the earth was "without form and void," and God starts to speak. The repeated phrase "And God said . . ." marks a sequence of creative and organizational steps by which God shapes the world and fills it with living creatures. In the final step God creates human beings in his image. They represent the pinnacle of God's creation: they alone are said to bear his image. Planet Earth is special. It was created with an ultimate purpose – that of having human beings on it.[8]

The Genesis narrative, therefore, is not just informing us how the universe came to exist; it is also saying why it came to exist. For this reason Genesis emphasizes not only the processes of creation but also God's organization of the universe in general and the earth in particular, so that it could function as a suitable home for men and women made in his image. Planet Earth has to be given a certain form – light separated from darkness, dry land from sea, visible lights in the sky, plant life to eat – in order for human life to thrive and function as God intended.

This biblical teaching – that the earth was specifically designed as a home for human beings – fits well with what contemporary science tells us about the fine-tuning of the universe. In recent years physicists and cosmologists have discovered that the fundamental constants of nature – those special numbers on which everything depends – have to be "just right" in order for life as we know it to be possible.[9] Lord Rees, the Astronomer Royal – who is not a theist – writes about this in his book *Just Six Numbers*. The Nobel Prize–winning physicist Arno Penzias comments on these remarkable findings: "Astronomy leads us to a unique event, a universe which was created out of nothing, one with the very delicate balance needed to provide exactly the right conditions required to permit life, and one which has an underlying (one might say 'supernatural') plan."[10] Paul Davies's testimony is again helpful: "I cannot believe that our existence in this universe is a mere quirk of fate, an accident of history, an incidental blip in the great cosmic drama. Our involvement is too intimate . . . We are truly meant to be here."[11]

So, both Genesis and science say that the universe is geared to supporting human life. But Genesis says more. It says that you as a human being bear the image of God. The starry heavens show the glory of God, yes; but they are not made in God's image. You are. That makes you unique. It gives you incalculable value. The galaxies are unimaginably large compared with you. However, you know that they exist, but they don't know that you exist. You are more significant, therefore, than a galaxy. Size is not necessarily a reliable measure of value, as any woman can tell you as she looks at the diamonds on her finger, and compares them with lumps of coal. Blaise Pascal said:

> Man is only a reed, the weakest in nature, but he is a thinking reed. There is no need for the whole universe to take up arms to crush him: a vapour, a drop of water is enough to kill him. But even if the universe were to crush him, man would still be nobler than his slayer, because he knows that he is dying and the advantage the universe has over him. The universe knows none of this.[12]

GOD CREATES BY HIS WORD

We have already seen that the fact that God did not do every-thing at once leads us to think that the purpose of God's creation of the earth was for it to be a home for the only beings that bear his image – namely, humans. The individual steps to reach that goal were initiated by God speaking: "And God said . . ." This repeated reference to the activity of the word of God in creation resonates very powerfully with me as a scientist. The idea that the universe did not come to be without the input of information and energy from an intelligent source seems to me to have been amply confirmed by scientific discovery.

Firstly, the language of mathematics has proved to be a powerful tool in describing how things work. Its codifications of the laws of nature into short and elegant "words" consisting of symbols surely reflect the greater Word that is ultimately responsible for the physical structures of the universe.

Secondly, above and beyond that, there is the major scientific discovery – one of the greatest of all time – that in each of the ten trillion cells of our body we humans possess a "word" of mind-boggling length, the human genome. This "word" is 3.5 billion "letters" long, written in the four chemical "letters" C, G, A, and T. Francis Crick and James Watson's Nobel Prize–winning discovery of the double-helix structure of the DNA that carries this genetic information has given rise to the molecular biology revolution

– the study of large, information-bearing macromolecules like DNA. More recently, it has been discovered that the genome is a read-write database that is used by the organism. This has introduced a whole new level of "epigenetic" complexity into molecular biology. It has also been found that an organism can modify its own genome, thus leading to modifications that may be inherited. Information abounds in the engineering miracle of the living cell to a much greater extent than hitherto realized.

In recent years, information has come to be regarded as one of the fundamental concepts of science. One of the most intriguing things about it is that it is not physical. The information you are reading at the moment is carried on the physical medium of paper and ink (or on a physical computer screen). But the information itself is not material. As I argue in detail elsewhere,[13] the non-materiality of information points to a non-material source – a mind, the mind of God.

On top of all that, we human beings have also been gifted with a phenomenal facility to use words to describe our universe and to communicate with each other. Does not this capacity point unmistakably to the vastly greater Word, who has endowed us with his image and imprint? Yet many people write off the claim that Christ is the Word of God as preposterous and impossible to accept in a scientifically literate age. As a scientist I must confess that I find their attitude very strange. After giving a lecture on "Science and God" to a large group of scientists at a major research establishment, I was (pleasantly) accosted by a physicist, who said, "I deduce from your lecture that you not only believe in God, but you are a Christian. You are therefore obliged to believe that Jesus Christ was simultaneously God and human. How can you, as a scientist, explain that?"

My reaction was to ask him a question as a quid pro quo. And as I regarded it as a simpler question, I suggested he answer first. "Agreed," he said.

"What is consciousness?" I asked.

"We don't really know," he responded.

"Never mind," I said. "Let's try something even simpler. What is energy?"

"Well," he replied, "we have equations governing it. We can measure it and use it."

"That wasn't my question! What *is* energy?"

After some thought, he said (as I knew he would), "We don't really know."

I then said, "Do you believe in consciousness and in energy?"

"Yes," he said.

"So you believe in them, and you do not know what they are? Should I write you off as a physicist?"

"Please don't," he pleaded.

I responded, "Yet you were prepared to write me off as a scientist unless I could explain something vastly more complex than consciousness or energy – the nature of God himself. Tell me," I went on, "why do you believe in consciousness and energy even though you don't understand what they are?"

"Well, I suppose it is because these concepts make sense. They have a kind of explanatory power, and you don't have to understand them completely in order to use them to explain other things."

"Precisely," I agreed. "And that is why I believe that Jesus was both man and God. I cannot explain it – by definition it must be one of the most difficult things of any to explain, far more difficult than consciousness or energy – but I believe it because it makes sense of everything else. It is the only interpretation that adequately accounts for Jesus' birth, life, death, resurrection, and ascension."[14]

GOD IS THE SOURCE OF LIGHT

The sequence of days begins with, "And God said, 'Let there be light.'" We have noted the fact that the sun and moon are not mentioned until day 4 and have considered some of the famous issues this raises. In order to deepen our understanding of what is going on here, we now refer to a key text in the New Testament that we have already used in connection with "creation by word" – John 1. John 1:1–5 reads:

> In the beginning was the Word, and the Word was with God, and the Word was God. He was in the beginning with God. All things were made through him, and

without him was not any thing made that was made. In him was life, and the life was the light of men. The light shines in the darkness, and the darkness has not overcome it.

John mentions light and darkness. Speaking of the Word, he says, "In him was life, and the life was the light of men." We are still talking about creation here. We have not yet reached the incarnation in John's narrative, nor his subsequent statement that Jesus is the light of the world. We need therefore to ask: In what sense is life a light?

Day 1 in Genesis 1 helps us here by telling us that light originated in a speech act of God. By speaking of light as such and not mentioning the sun, the text opens our thinking to a rich spectrum of ideas. John connects light with life. If we are on a ship and see the beam of a lighthouse, we immediately ask: What is its source? Where is it coming from? That is, in a metaphorical sense, we are asking for light on that particular light. And life, all life, has that effect – particularly on biologists! They put enormous resources into their search for light on life: Where does it come from?

There is a powerful message here for the contemporary world. If we do not include God the Word in our search for light on life, we shall end up in darkness. It is fascinating to live at the time in history when scientists shone a powerful light on the structure of DNA and discovered it was a word, an unmistakable indication of its ultimate origin.

The New Testament draws even more from day 1. In a

famous passage, Paul makes an analogy between this statement and the proclamation of the Christian message: "For what we proclaim is not ourselves, but Jesus Christ as Lord, with ourselves as your servants for Jesus' sake. For God, who said, 'Let light shine out of darkness,' has shone in our hearts to give the light of the knowledge of the glory of God in the face of Jesus Christ" (2 Corinthians 4:5–6).

Paul uses creation as a *metaphor* for what happens to a person at conversion. Once more it is worth stressing that the metaphor denotes something real at a deeper level than the merely physical. The light that God shines into the human heart that trusts him is not physical, of course, but it is real. It is not a matter of mere psychological wishful thinking. The gospel effects an actual spiritual transformation, as Paul goes on to say in the very next chapter, again using the language of creation: "If anyone is in Christ, he is a new creation. The old has passed away; behold, the new has come" (2 Corinthians 5:17). It is for this reason that we can have confidence in the Christian message – it brings real illumination, authenticating itself in human experience. It also authenticates itself intellectually, as C. S. Lewis pointed out: "I believe in Christianity as I believe that the Sun has risen, not only because I see it, but because by it I see everything else."[15]

There is even more in the New Testament about this matter of creation light. In fact, Jesus himself refers to the very first occurrence of the word *day* in Genesis and draws from it a surprising and powerful application to our lives.

John relates this application in his gospel as one of the major signs that Jesus performed to confirm his claim to be the Son of God, the Word of God incarnate. It is the famous story of the raising of Lazarus from the dead (John 11:1–12:11). Lazarus lived with his sisters Mary and Martha in the village of Bethany, near Jerusalem. Lazarus fell ill, and the sisters sent a message to Jesus, who had become a friend of the family. Jesus did not respond at once but remained for two days where he was with his disciples. He then announced to them that he intended to go back to Judea, since Lazarus was sick. Later Jesus explained to them that he was going in order to awaken Lazarus from the "sleep" of death.

The disciples reacted to Jesus' announcement very negatively: "Rabbi, the Jews were just now seeking to stone you, and are you going there again?" (John 11:8). To the disciples, a trip back to Judea at that time seemed suicidal. In Perea, north of the Dead Sea, far from Jerusalem, they felt safe, but such was the antagonism that had arisen against Jesus that they were afraid of what might happen if they appeared in or near the capital.

Jesus answered them by referring to the construction of what we call the solar system: "Are there not twelve hours in the day? If anyone walks in the day, he does not stumble, because he sees the light of this world. But if anyone walks in the night, he stumbles, because *the light is not in him*" (John 11:9–10, emphasis added). Jesus was concerned to teach his disciples an important lesson from the very arrangement of the lighting system for our world, as first described in

Genesis 1. The lesson is based on the first mention of the word *day*: "God called the light Day, and the darkness he called Night" (Genesis 1:5). One could easily miss the fact that it is God who gives the name "day" to the light. Genesis is a book in which God tells humans to get on with the job of naming things, so why does God reserve to himself the giving of names to just a few, a very few, aspects of the created universe? It certainly has the effect of drawing them to our attention, for day and light are not quite the same thing, are they?

Jesus here explains something very important that is easy to miss – the organization of the world as distinct from its creation.[16] God's calling of the light "day" and his calling of the darkness "night" are not creative acts in the strict sense. They are organizational. What enables the linguistic distinction to be made is nothing less than the geometrical arrangement of the solar system.

In order to achieve this arrangement, firstly, the source of light for our planet, the sun, has to be physically situated outside our planet home. As Jesus says, referring now to day 4 of Genesis, the light is not in us. Secondly, earth has to rotate on its own axis, constantly presenting a different face to the sun, so that each earth rotation is divided up into hours of daylight and hours of night. In that sense, day is our experience of the light (of the sun). The light is rationed by the deliberate strategy of the Creator himself.

In day 4 in Genesis, we find a description of what the sun, moon, and stars are for. The Genesis text tells us explicitly:

"Let them be for signs and for seasons, and for days and years" (1:14).

In this technological age, those of us who live in cities easily forget the fundamental role played by the sun, moon, and stars in the organization of life on earth. But for millennia, people were dependent on seeing these "lights" in the sky, not only to determine the cycles of seedtime and harvest – the times to have their animals graze on the mountains or in the valleys, vital to the sustenance of life – but also to navigate. Those "lights" help humans find their place and time in space-time.

The conversation between Jesus and his disciples that took place in an obscure country tucked away in a corner of the vast Roman Empire twenty centuries ago now takes on an awe-inspiring dimension. The man who addressed the group of disciples that day was none other than the Creator, the Word through whom all things came to exist. He himself was the architect and creator of the solar system about which he was speaking. It was his divine mind that had conceived of the idea of a vast nuclear furnace rolling through trackless space, warping space-time around it and thus holding earth captive in its orbit and bathed in its light and heat. It was his idea to put the source of light outside the world on which he would later place his supreme creation, men and women made in his image. And here he was, the Creator, standing on his specially designed planet Earth, deigning to explain to a group of his human creatures why he had organized the solar system that way. I think we ought to listen, don't you?

The disciples thought that if they followed Jesus back to Judea it would be suicidal. They would be safe only if they remained where they were. To them this was a matter of simple logic. The authorities in Jerusalem were out to get Jesus, so the safest place for the disciples, they thought, was at a maximum distance from the capital, far away in the provinces. That idea came from inside their heads, of course. That is, they were relying for their guidance on a source of light inside them. But that is not what they did when it came to walking around the countryside. They would travel in daylight, dependent on the external light of the sun. At night they would stumble and be unable to find the way, since *the light was not in them.*

They probably did not know, as we know now, that there are certain marine creatures with a light in them. Bioluminescent fish,[17] for instance, produce light by chemical means, and some of them use their light for navigation. Humans are not made that way. They depend on a source of light that not only is not in them; it is not even in their world.[18] The earth was deliberately built that way, spinning round its star 150,000,000 kilometres (more than 93,000,000 miles) away, a star on which it is utterly dependent for its light, heat, and energy.

Jesus is, of course, using the arrangement of earth's illumination as a vivid metaphor for something at another level entirely. He expected his disciples to deduce something simple yet profound from his observation about the sun: If in the physical realm they were helplessly dependent on a light situated outside themselves, what about the intellectual, spiritual, and moral realms? Where was the source of their insights and answers, inside or outside their own heads?

This question has lost none of its relevance. The battle between the worldviews of theism and naturalism is about whether or not there is an outside to get guidance from. To the atheist, this universe is a closed system of cause and effect that is ultimately self-explanatory in terms of its basic physics and chemistry, its matter and energy. The only source of wisdom for atheists is from within their own heads.

By contrast, to the biblical theist, this universe is an open system – neither self-existent nor self-explanatory. There is a source of wisdom outside the whole system – namely, God. This means, for instance, that just as our earth depends on the external sun for its light so that we cannot even see our planet properly without that light, at the higher level any final explanation of the universe and human beings that does not include God will unravel into darkness. It is for this reason, too, that naturalistic attempts to explain the existence of life solely in terms of the nonliving, of consciousness in terms of the unconscious, of the rational in terms of the nonrational, of human beings solely in terms of animals, of morality in terms of the dictates of pain and pleasure, are bound to fail in the end. The sad irony of the Enlightenment is that it puts the light inside man by making human reason the ultimate arbiter.

So much for the philosophical level. Jesus' words about light and the sun, however, were addressed not to scientists or philosophers but to a group of ordinary men who were fearful about their physical security. The lesson was for them in the first instance. They had perhaps forgotten something that Jesus had already taught them. On a previous visit to Jerusalem, he had made another profound statement about light: "I am the light of the world. Whoever follows me will not walk in darkness, but will have the light of life" (John 8:12). That is, Jesus himself is a source of light. Not just any source of light; he is *the* source of light for the world. This is an astonishing statement, parallel to his later claim: "I am . . . the truth" (John 14:6).

Those of us who are scientists like to think that, somewhere along the line, we have shed at least some little light on a problem, often a very obscure problem, and thus advanced the cause of knowledge in a modest way. A few scientists have had the privilege of shedding light on hitherto intractable human problems, and their solutions have brought great benefit – the discovery of penicillin, for instance. But no scientist in his or her right mind would ever dream of claiming to be *the* light. Jesus did – and he gave evidence by his life, death, and resurrection that the claim was true.

Furthermore, Jesus implied that he was a *moving* source of light. It is obvious that if a light is moving, it will benefit you only if you keep pace with it. It is the same with Jesus. In order to stay in his light and have it illuminate our path, we must keep in step with him: "Whoever follows me . . . will have the light of life."

The challenge to the disciples was clear. Without any

light coming from God on this issue, their human reason would tell them that they were walking to their deaths. But Jesus said that if they followed him, a travelling light that was external to them, they would discover that he was the very light of life. How much of this they understood at the time we do not know. What we do know is that they followed him, but, by Thomas at least, it was done in a mood of reluctant pessimism: "Let us also go, that we may die with him" (John 11:16). At least they went. And it was good that they did.

The journey led to a graveyard in Bethany, where Lazarus, already four days dead, lay interred in a Middle Eastern tomb, mourned by his sisters. Jesus announced to Martha that her brother, Lazarus, would rise again. She replied that she fully expected him to rise at the final resurrection at the last day. Upon hearing his, Jesus made a further astounding statement: "I am the resurrection and the life. Whoever believes in me, though he die, yet shall he live, and everyone who lives and believes in me shall never die. Do you believe this?" (John 11:25–26). With remarkable composure she replied, "Yes, Lord; I believe that you are the Christ, the Son of God, who is coming into the world" (11:27).

It was not long before Martha's faith was vindicated. Jesus ordered the stone covering the mouth of the tomb to be removed, against the humanly reasonable protest by Martha that there would be an awful smell. He then commanded Lazarus to come out. And Lazarus, bound with graveclothes, did just that. It was a spectacular vindication of Jesus' claim to be the resurrection and the life. For the disciples it put death into a different light. The Jesus they followed had power over death. They would never think of death in the same way again. Nor should we.

But there was another side. The sisters had sent a message, counting on Jesus' love for the family. They assumed he would come and heal Lazarus. And when he arrived late, they remonstrated a little: "Lord, if you had been here, my brother would not have died" (John 11:21, 32). They had been relying on what seemed reasonable in purely human terms, and it nearly caused them to doubt the love Jesus had for them. Life's circumstances often do that to us. Sometimes we try to use our powers of reason to make sense of what has happened, and in our trying we fail. We need light from outside.

There are, of course, no easy answers here, though one thing is clear: atheism has no hope to give. It has no light to shed on death. For atheism, death is the ultimate darkness. But Jesus has shown that death is not the end. Furthermore, for those who trust him as Lord and Saviour, there is to be a joyful resurrection. The evidence for that is not so much that Jesus raised Lazarus but that Jesus himself rose on the third day and showed himself to many witnesses (1 Corinthians 15:1–11).

THE GOODNESS OF CREATION

One cannot read Genesis 1 without noticing the constant refrain, "And God saw that it was good" (verses 4, 10, 12,

18, 21, 25), culminating in the final assessment on day 6: "And God saw everything that he had made, and behold, it was very good" (1:31). God is not some distant deistic figure uninterested in his work. He regards his creation with the enthusiasm and joy of a skillful artist who is delighted at what he has done as he sees it formed and organized step by step, until the wonderful harmony of his completed work lies before him, thoroughly fit for the glorious purpose for which he intended it.

Sadly, it would not be long before the original harmony of creation was disrupted, as the first humans failed at the higher level of moral goodness, and sin entered the world to wreak endless havoc. So serious is that moral infection that the business of restoring men and women to fellowship with their Creator will involve something much bigger than creation itself – nothing less than the Creator becoming human, dying at the hands of his creatures, and rising again in triumph over sin and death.

Yet at the beginning all was perfect. How different from pantheistic philosophies that regarded matter as essentially evil and held that our wisdom would be to escape from it completely. Indeed, just as the material creation was originally perfect, one day there will be a new creation – a new heaven and a new earth that will also be perfect, and righteousness will dwell in them (see 2 Peter 3:13; Revelation 21).

In the meantime, the fact that God has put human beings in charge of a good creation reminds us also of our responsibility towards God as stewards of creation. It is not our property, but God's. We are not at liberty to abuse, waste, and ruin it. Indeed, God takes our attitude towards the earth very seriously, as a day will come in which God will judge those who destroy the earth (Revelation 11:18).

THE SABBATH

Genesis 1 has much more to teach, but we shall content ourselves by concluding, appropriately enough, with some comments on the Sabbath. Leon Kass reminds us that the Mesopotamians and Babylonians had seven-day cycles that were associated with the phases of the moon, and they had their own *Sabattu*, the day of the full moon, which was a day of fasting and ill luck.[19]

Kass writes: "In contrast, the seventh day among the children of Israel was completely independent of all ties to the heavens, save to the Creator of heaven. It established a calendar completely dissociated from the cycles of the heavenly bodies,[20] commemorating instead their Creator, one who stands above and beyond their ceaseless motion."[21] Thus the institution of the Sabbath would remind us of the ever-present danger of human beings becoming subservient to the creation rather than the Creator (Romans 1:25).

The New Testament mentions the Sabbath in several contexts. We shall select just one, in which the concept of Sabbath is used to help us grasp a fundamental Christian doctrine that is often misunderstood. The writer to the Hebrews cites the Sabbath passage from Genesis 1 and, after a lengthy discussion of the nature of rest, concludes by saying, "There remains a Sabbath rest for the people of God, for whoever has entered God's rest has also rested from his works as God did from his" (Hebrews 4:9–10).

Here, once more, a biblical author uses a concept from Genesis as a metaphor for something real at a deeper level. In this passage, "as God did from his" refers to the work of creation from which God rested on the seventh day. God did the creating, and then he rested from it. We inherit a universe that we did not create.

It is important, particularly for those of us who are scientists, to remind ourselves of this fact from time to time. We did not put the universe there. We did not create the objects of scientific study. We study something given. This simple idea has consequences. It means, for instance, that it is for the universe to shape our ideas about how it works rather than for us to decide in our heads how it ought to work and then force the universe to comply. We all need to be reminded of this and the general principle it enshrines. Former British Chief Rabbi Jonathan Sacks writes of the Sabbath: "It is a day that sets a limit to our intervention in nature and to our economic activity. We become conscious of being creations, not creators. The earth is not ours, but God's . . . The Sabbath is a weekly reminder of the integrity of nature and the boundaries of human striving."[22]

It is those "boundaries of human striving" with which the passage in Hebrews is concerned. All of us long for rest. Not simply the taking of a regular day of rest and recuperation, or going on a much-needed holiday, but respite from the constant pressure to achieve. That pressure turns some people into workaholics, driven by an unreachable goal of the achievement that would give them, they hope, some enduring significance. But there are other things that make us restless – loneliness, broken relationships, frustration, unfulfilled desires, guilt, pain, illness, hurt, burdens of family and friends, and a multitude of other things. We are restless beings. Augustine of Hippo long ago traced the reason for this back to creation: "[O Lord,] You have made us for Yourself, and our hearts are restless until they rest in You."[23]

Augustine was surely thinking of the solution to this restlessness that was given by Jesus himself: "Come to me, all who labor and are heavy laden, and I will give you rest. Take my yoke upon you, and learn from me, for I am gentle and lowly in heart, and you will find rest for your souls. For my yoke is easy, and my burden is light" (Matthew 11:28–30).

Jesus' invitation is clear. That rest comes when we are prepared to come to him and accept what he calls his "yoke," that is, his authority and leadership. At the heart of Christianity is a willingness to trust Jesus Christ as Lord and Saviour and thereby receive forgiveness and peace with God. The problem is that in a world where achievement and merit count for so much, we human beings find it difficult to understand and accept that God's forgiveness and peace cannot be earned by our work, effort, or merit, but must be received as a free gift.

And that, says the letter to Hebrews, is where the Sabbath can help us. Not now at the level of resting one day in seven, but in understanding the principle that is involved. God did the work of creating the universe, and then he rested. We inherit a creation that we didn't work for, merit, or earn. In that sense, we rest in what God has done. Entering God's spiritual rest – receiving his forgiveness, salvation, and peace – proceeds in exactly the same way. God has completed the work on which salvation rests: the death of Jesus for human sin on the cross. In order to enter God's rest, we must rest on the work that Jesus has done, not on the work we do. Paul makes this principle crystal clear: "Now to the one who works, his wages are not counted as a gift but as his due. And to the one who does not work but believes in him who justifies the ungodly, his faith is counted as righteousness" (Romans 4:4–5).

BACK TO THE BEGINNING: A PERSONAL NOTE

It is now over forty years since I was married. In our wedding service, Sally and I were addressed by an extraordinary man. In his youth he had been a heavyweight boxer of the sort who took on all comers at fairgrounds. When he became a Christian, his life took on a markedly different character. He went back to school as an adult and sat with the children to try to catch up on his education. He had a prodigious memory and was able to develop an encyclopedic knowledge of the Bible, which he then used to great effect in communicating the Christian faith to everyone from shipyard workers to Cambridge students, all of whom loved him for his directness and honesty. His name was Stan Ford.

His wedding address centered on the text, "In the beginning, God created the heavens and the earth." Stan was no scientist, though he respected learning. But the point he made that day has reverberated powerfully through our married life. It was based on the first four words of his text: "In the beginning, God . . ." A wedding was a new beginning, he said, and there would be many other new beginnings in the future. The foundation for every new beginning was that God should be in on it. We have proved him right. What would a beginning be without God? The universe itself couldn't have started without him.

If some of this sounds too much like preaching, just remember that we are not critical of people who are passionate about science or football! In any case, I don't think it will do any harm. It is one thing to wrestle with the meaning of the days of Genesis; it is another to understand, apply, and live the whole message of Genesis. And if we are not doing the latter, I am not sure that the former will profit us much.

Come to think of it, I never did ask Stan about the days. Too late now. The irony is that he now knows much more about them than I do, or ever will – in this life.

What, therefore, should our attitude be towards others who do not agree with us, whatever view we hold? Surely the old adage has got it more or less right: "In essentials, unity; in nonessentials, liberty; and in all things, charity."

But there we really must let matters rest! It is high time for a Sabbath!

NOTES

1. Furthermore, the biblical worldview best explains why science is possible; see John C. Lennox, *Cosmic Chemistry: Do God and Science Mix?* (Oxford: Lion Hudson, 2021), part 2.

2. A figure of speech in which a totality is expressed by referring to its contrasting parts. Another example of this in Genesis is the phrase "the knowledge of good and evil," which, it is suggested, is a merism for "the knowledge of everything."

3. Stephen Hawking, "The Beginning of Time," http://homepages.wmich.edu/~korista/hawking-time.html.

4. Note that this analogy applies to the manner rather than the timing of creation, since the timing is part of the standard (big bang) model.

5. See appendix A.

6. For more on this, see my *God and Stephen Hawking*, 2nd ed. (Oxford: Lion Hudson, 2021).

7. Although the word *Trinity* does not appear in the New Testament, Thomas Torrance has pointed out that the doctrine of the Trinity is not so much a Christian formulation as it is the way that God has revealed himself (see his *The Christian Doctrine of God: One Being, Three Persons* (Edinburgh: T&T Clark, 1996).

8. It is therefore fitting that the description of the sixth day is longer than that of the other days.

9. See Lennox, *God and Stephen Hawking*, 51.

10. Arno Penzias, "Creation Is Supported by All the Data So Far," in *Cosmos, Bios, Theos: Scientists Reflect on Science, God, and the Origins of the Universe, Life, and Homo Sapiens*, ed. Henry Margenau and Roy A. Varghese (La Salle, IL: Open Court, 1992), 83.

11. Paul Davies, *The Mind of God: The Scientific Basis for a Rational World* (London: Simon & Schuster, 1992), 232.

12. Quoted in Peter Kreeft, *Christianity for Modern Pagans: Pascal's Pensées Edited, Outlined and Explained* (San Francisco: Ignatius, 1993), 55.

13. See Lennox, *Cosmic Chemistry*, chapter 21.

14. For the related objection that science and miracles are incompatible, see

John C. Lennox, *Gunning for God: Why the New Atheists Are Missing the Target* (Oxford: Lion Hudson, 2011), 165–86.

15. C. S. Lewis, *The Weight of Glory and Other Addresses* (1945; repr., New York: HarperCollins, 2001), 140.

16. This emphasis was first pointed out to me by Professor David Gooding.

17. Biologist Andrew Parker, author of *The Genesis Enigma* (London: Doubleday, 2009), is a world authority in this field.

18. If the sun were to be extinguished, human life would not survive for long – even with artificial sources of light and heat.

19. See Gordon J. Wenham, *Genesis 1–15*, Word Biblical Commentary 1 (Waco, TX: Word, 1987), 35, who suggests that the Sabbath may have been introduced as a deliberate counterblast to the Mesopotamian lunar-regulated cycle.

20. It is good to remind ourselves of this, since our English names of the days of the week are derived from the names of planets and pagan deities.

21. Leon Kass, *The Beginning of Wisdom* (Chicago: University of Chicago Press, 2006), 52.

22. Jonathan Sacks, *The Dignity of Difference: How to Avoid the Clash of Civilizations* (New York: Continuum, 2002), 167.

23. Augustine, *The Confessions*, book 1, chapter 1, New Advent, www.newadvent.org/fathers/110101.htm.

A BRIEF BACKGROUND TO GENESIS

The book of Genesis was originally written in Hebrew, and its title in that language comes from the very first word in the text, *bereš'it*, which means "in the beginning."[1] The title "Genesis" (Greek for "origin") was given to the book by its early Greek translators.

Edward J. Young, a distinguished Hebrew scholar, says that the text has the marks of a prose narrative describing a succession of events. It lacks a major characteristic of Hebrew poetry – namely, two-line parallelism, where a statement is made on one line and then repeated in different words on the next line. For example:

> To you, O Lord, I cry,
> > and to the Lord I plead for mercy.
>
> *Psalm 30:8*

However, Young also points out that Genesis 1 has certain features that would be unusual in straight prose. For example, it contains repeated refrains like "and God saw that it was good," and repetitions like "And God said," "let there be," and "and it was so." Hence the impression given is of a text that is written in "exalted, semi-poetical language," in the sense that it features certain semi-poetical elements that serve to make it memorable but do not take away from an ordered narrative purpose.[2] Indeed, the phrases mentioned above serve to introduce what are clearly nonpoetic factual statements about the creation and organization of the physical universe itself.

Regarding the genre of Genesis 1, C. John Collins writes: "We have called the passage a narrative, and this is proper because of the prominent use of the *wayyiqtol*[3] to denote successive events. But we must acknowledge that it is an unusual narrative indeed: not only because of the unique events described and the lack of other actors besides God, but also because of the highly patterned way of telling it all."[4]

The Genesis text comes to us from the ancient Near East, and so any attempt to understand it will be enriched by knowledge of the literature and culture of the time. But what culture, at what time? Genesis talks about the foundation of the great cities of the ancient Near East in Mesopotamia, and it describes the pilgrimage of Abraham from Ur of the Chaldeans to Canaan and the life of his children in Canaan, followed by the movement of his family to Egypt. Thus the cultures of Mesopotamia, Canaan, and Egypt come into the picture. Traditionally, although Moses's name is not mentioned in the book, the authorship of Genesis is ascribed to him, and Genesis is often called the First Book of Moses.[5] This would mean that it dates from somewhere around the fifteenth to thirteenth centuries BC.

As to how the Genesis text was understood by those living in the culture that it ultimately generated, we have the evidence of the Old and New Testaments to show us that they took the Genesis material as history. The Jewish historian Josephus, in his introduction to his famous *Jewish Antiquities*, written around AD 110, demonstrates an acute awareness of the difference between a carefully researched factual account of history, on the one hand, and fables and deliberate fabrications, on the other.

In this regard it is interesting to compare the Genesis account with the literature of contemporary ancient cultures. One important example is the Babylonian epic *Enuma Elish*, whose title means "When on high," translating the first two words of this epic that was written in the Old Babylonian period[6] (second millennium BC) and completed about 1000 BC, according to ancient Near Eastern scholar K. A. Kitchen.[7]

Enuma Elish was a story of great cultural importance among the Babylonians, and its recitation by the priests formed the centrepiece of the fourth day of the annual New Year festival. However, *Enuma Elish* is not so much an account of creation as the story of war among the Babylonian gods. It relates how the god Marduk gained his supremacy, with creation as a by-product of his battle. Marduk defeated the goddess Ti'amat and split her body into two pieces. With one piece he made the earth, and with the other the sky. In the Babylonian account, then, creation is secondary; the gods and their wars take centre stage.[8] Here are the first few lines to give the flavour of the epic:

> When on high the heaven had not been named,
> Firm ground below had not been called by name,
> Naught but primordial Apsu, their begetter.
> (And) Mummu [and?] Tiamat, she who bore them all,
> Their waters commingling as a single body;
> No reed hut had been matted, no marsh land had
>   appeared;
> When no gods whatever had been brought into being,
> Uncalled by name, their destinies undetermined –
> Then it was that the gods were formed within them.[9]

Attention has been drawn to certain similarities between the Genesis account and *Enuma Elish*. For instance, *Enuma Elish* is written on seven tablets, and the Genesis account speaks of seven days; there is a similar order of creation – heavens, sea, and earth; and in the sixth tablet, as on the sixth day, human beings are created.

These correspondences have led some scholars to surmise that the Genesis account is derived from the Babylonian *Enuma Elish* (and, arguing similarly, that the Genesis narrative of the flood derives from the *Epic of Gilgamesh* and the *Atrahasis* epic[10]). They think that the idea of God transforming an initial chaos into a cosmos is a throwback, not simply to an early state of the universe, but to myths concerning a primeval chaotic power that was pitted against the gods. Some additionally hold that these dependencies show that Genesis is of comparatively late date, having been composed in the time of the Jewish exile in Babylon in the sixth century BC.[11]

However, many scholars point out that the surface similarities mask much more significant differences. Most striking is the fact that Genesis lacks the central theme of the Babylonian epic, theogony, that is, an account of the genesis of the gods, which is a common characteristic of ancient Near Eastern mythologies.[12] The God of Genesis is utterly distinct. He was not created by the universe, as were the pagan gods. It is the other way round. The God of Genesis is not a created God at all; he is the Creator of the universe.

Furthermore, according to Genesis, human beings are created in the image of God as the pinnacle of his creation: "Let us make man in our own image"; according to the *Enuma Elish*, in contrast, human beings are created as an afterthought to lighten the work of the gods:

> I will establish a savage, "man" shall be his name,
> Verily, savage man I will create,
> He shall be charged with the service of the gods
> That they might be at ease![13]

Also, in contrast with the Mesopotamian myths, Genesis has no multiplicity of warring gods and goddesses; the heavens and earth are not made out of a god; there are no mythical beasts; and, strikingly, there are no deifications of stars, planets, sun, and moon – the usual names of the last two are not even used in Genesis 1.

The universe to which Genesis introduces us is no mythical construct; it is our familiar world, with light, sky, sea, and land; sun, moon, and stars; plants, fish, and animals; and human beings. Genesis is concerned with actual and not mythical events in the world. And over it all, God the Creator presides, speaking his creative word so that all is accomplished. If Genesis depends on the Babylonian account, as is claimed, why then is it so utterly different from that account? Its assertion that there is only one God, the Creator who is distinct from his creation, stands in direct contradiction to the idolatrous interpretations of the universe that lie at the heart of the polytheistic mythologies of Babylon and elsewhere.[14] By ascribing creation to one supreme God who is not himself part of creation, Genesis protests by its very nature against such polytheism.[15] For instance, ascribing to the sun the humble role of light bearer rather than god would be a powerful challenge to the mythology of the land of Joseph's rule and of Moses's upbringing, where the supreme god was the sun god Ra, whose name was embedded in the title of the ruler Pha-*ra*-oh.

One response to this paradoxical situation is the suggestion that an original mythological text has undergone a process of gradual de-deification – a removal of the mythological gods and ideas in order to turn it into a protest against the idolatry of Babylon that so grieved the Jews in exile.[16] However, K. A. Kitchen disagrees: "The common assumption that the Hebrew account is simply a purged and simplified version of the Babylonian legend (applied also to the flood stories) is fallacious on methodological grounds. In the Ancient Near East, the rule is that simple accounts or traditions may give rise (by accretion and embellishment) to elaborate legends, but not vice versa. In the Ancient Orient, legends were not simplified or turned into pseudo-history (historicized) as has been assumed for early Genesis."[17]

In any case, no de-deification took place for the simple reason that there was no need for it. The Genesis account was written by someone who never did believe in a multiplicity of gods in the first place.

The idea of the book being a product of substantial revision and reinterpretation of earlier mythologies is also rejected by Alan Millard, who discovered and deciphered one of the ancient Babylonian flood texts that had been left forgotten in a drawer in the British Museum. Millard points out: "It has yet to be shown that there was borrowing, even indirectly . . . All who suspect or suggest borrowing by the Hebrews are compelled to admit large-scale revision, alteration, and reinterpretation in a fashion which cannot be substantiated for any other composition from the Ancient Near East or in any other Hebrew writing."[18]

More recently, Kitchen argues that although there are

analogies between the contents of Genesis 1–11 and the rich literary heritage from the ancient Near East, in the sense that the Genesis narratives also speak of creation and a flood,[19] there is no direct relationship between Genesis and these other traditions: "Despite the reiterated claims of an older generation of biblical scholars, *Enuma Elish* and Gen. 1–2 in fact share no direct relationship. Thus the word *tehom/thm* is common to both Hebrew and Ugaritic (north Syrian), and means nothing more than 'deep, abyss.' It is not a deity, like Ti'amat, a goddess in *Enuma Elish*."[20] Elsewhere he sums up: "The attempts made in the past to establish a definite relationship between Genesis and Babylonian epics such as *Enuma Elish* have now had to be abandoned; in content, aim, theology and philology there is divergence and no proven link."[21]

This brings us back to the matter of dating. Kitchen points out several strands of evidence that converge on an early date:

1. The topic of the division of languages mentioned in Genesis 11 is very old – it is also recorded in a nineteenth-/eighteenth-century Sumerian composition in relation to a king who lived around 2600 BC.
2. The kind of structure exhibited by Genesis 1–11 is not known in the ancient Near East after 1600 BC and is characteristic of documents before that time.
3. The scribal use of cuneiform script spread from

Mesopotamia as far as Canaan, Hazor, and even Hebron by the seventeenth century BC, so that the account could have been written as early as that time.

Kitchen sums up the evidence as follows:

So no objection can be taken to the essence of Genesis 1–11 going westward at this epoch; its written formulation in early Hebrew may then have followed later and independently. The patriarchal tradition would then have been passed down in Egypt (as family tradition) to the fourteenth/thirteenth century, possibly then first put into writing . . . It is part of the oldest levels of Hebrew tradition, as were the Mesopotamian accounts in their culture.

As to biblical records of creation that do have a later date, Kitchen adds:

In biblical terms the Genesis 1–11 account stands in sharpest contrast with the only other extensive Hebrew account of origins, which began from the beginning – by that indubitably postexilic writer, the Chronicler, from circa 430 . . . It is noteworthy that he did not give a later version of creation, fall, and flood, etc., but simply summed up baldly the entire "history" from Adam to Abraham genealogically in just the first part of a chapter

(1 Chronicles 1:1–28). Fashions had changed radically between the nineteenth and the fifth centuries in this regard as well as in so much else in ancient life.[22]

By now the attentive reader may be asking how the date of composition of the original text of Genesis can have any real importance, since the polytheisms of the time of Moses were not, after all, much different from those of the period of the Jewish Babylonian exile. Placing the main emphasis on the polytheistic background (which the text itself does not explicitly mention) can take attention away from the foreground, the matter of origins (which the text does explicitly mention). For instance, it is frequently suggested that the text of Genesis is theological and literary, as distinct from historical or scientific, as if these are the only categories that should be considered, or, perhaps more importantly, as if they are mutually exclusive categories. It is, however, perfectly possible for a text simultaneously to inform us about objective facts and to have a theological purpose. Genesis does precisely that. In the words of C. John Collins: "Genesis is offering us the true story of mankind's past."[23]

NOTES

1. This usage is very ancient and was common in the ancient Semitic world from the eighteenth century BC (see Kenneth A. Kitchen, "The Old Testament in Its Context: Part 1," *Theological Students' Fellowship Bulletin* 59 [Spring 1971]: 9–10).

2. See Edward J. Young, *Studies in Genesis One* (Philadelphia: P&R, 1964), 82–83.

3. A Hebrew verbal form.

4. C. John Collins, *Genesis 1–4* (Phillipsburg, NJ: P&R, 2006), 43.

5. In German, for example.

6. See Georges Roux, *Ancient Iraq*, rev. ed. (1964; repr., London: Penguin, 1992), 95.

7. See K. A. Kitchen, *On the Reliability of the Old Testament* (Grand Rapids: Eerdmans, 2003), 424.

8. Kitchen writes: "In terms of theme, creation is the massively central concern of Gen. 1–2, but it is a mere tailpiece in *Enuma Elish*, which is dedicated to portraying the supremacy of the god Marduk of Babylon" (*On the Reliability*, 424).

9. "The Babylonian Epic of Creation: 'When on High,'" Academy for Ancient Texts, www.ancienttexts.org/library/mesopotamian/enuma.html.

10. Dating from the first half of the second millennium BC (See Kitchen, *On the Reliability*, 423).

11. Often on the basis of the largely abandoned documentary hypothesis that was popular in the first part of the last century.

12. Such theogonies typically describe how the gods are generated from primeval matter so that the gods are, in contemporary terminology, deifications of nature and its powers. These gods were thus "material" gods, which means that such ancient worldviews stand much closer to contemporary materialism than it might first appear.

13. "The Babylonian Epic of Creation: 'When on High.'"

14. There are major similarities between the polytheisms of Assyria, Egypt, Canaan, and Babylon.

15. Paul protests against the idolatry of the Athenians, using precisely this argument from creation (see Acts 17:22–25).

16. Analogous to the de-deification of the universe that was necessary in Greek thought, in order for scientific thinking to begin.

17. K. A. Kitchen, *Ancient Orient and Old Testament* (London: Tyndale, 1966), 89.

18. Alan Millard, "A New Babylonian 'Genesis' Story," in *I Studied Inscriptions from before the Flood: Ancient Near Eastern, Literary, and Linguistic Approaches to Genesis 1–11*, ed. Richard S. Hess and David Toshio Tsumura (Winona Lake, IN: Eisenbrauns, 1994), 127.

19. It should be mentioned that parallel traditions are evidence that there was a common event that triggered them. For instance, the famous Sumerian King List gives a list of kings and dynasties before the flood, then the flood, and then a long

sequence of post-diluvian dynasties. This document dates to the twentieth to nineteenth centuries BC. Kitchen makes the point, "The importance of this document for our purpose is that it shows the Sumero-Babylonian conviction that a specific flood once interrupted the course of their very earliest history and was ipso facto a historical event in their reckoning. Therefore, on that showing the event attested also by Genesis and the epics belongs to 'proto-history,' not to myth" (see Kitchen, "Old Testament in Its Context: Part 1," 3).

20. Kitchen, *On the Reliability*, 424.

21. Kitchen, "Old Testament in Its Context: Part 1," 3.

22. Kitchen, *On the Reliability*, 427.

23. Collins, *Genesis 1–4*, 243.

APPENDIX B

THE BEGINNING ACCORDING TO GENESIS AND SCIENCE

Though, for the most part, Scripture is concerned with matters arguably more important than science – the why of the meaning of existence, for instance, as distinct from the how of the laws and mechanisms governing the universe – nevertheless there is an important overlap. Perhaps the most important example of that overlap is the fact that both the Bible and science claim that the universe had a beginning. What is striking is that the Bible claimed it for thousands of years, whereas scientists only recently began even to entertain the possibility that there might have been a beginning. Aristotle's view – that the universe was eternal – dominated scientific thinking for hundreds of years without appreciable challenge.

Richard Dawkins was not impressed when I mentioned to him in one of our debates that the Bible was right about the universe having a beginning. He said that since there either was a beginning or was not, the Bible had a 50 percent chance to get it right – no big deal. But it *was* a big deal. For when scientific evidence began to indicate that the universe had not existed eternally, some leading scientists put up fierce resistance because they thought it would give too much support to those who believed in creation![1] It was not a question of guesswork. Those resisting scientific advance because they feared it supported the biblical worldview did not get their way, as the scientific evidence for a beginning proved too strong.

"In the beginning, God created the heavens and the earth." These magnificent opening words of the Bible have been much studied. The definite article attached to "beginning" in the translation is missing in Hebrew. This circumstance is understood by some as having the effect of shrouding the beginning in mystery. Leon Kass, for instance, writes: "About this, too, modern cosmology cannot help but agree: 'What was there before the big bang?' God only knows. Despite all our sophistication, the utter mysteriousness of the *ultimate* beginning and its source or cause cannot be eradicated."[2] However, C. John Collins points out that "the article is missing [from the word *beginning*] because the word is definite on its own."[3] Of course, from the perspective of physics, if God created time with space – space-time – then the word *before* is meaningless.

Let's sit back for a moment and listen to Bill Bryson, in his inimitable style, giving a popular scientific account of the beginning:

And so, from nothing, our universe begins.

In a single blinding pulse, a moment of glory much too swift and expansive for any form of words, the singularity assumes heavenly dimensions, space beyond conception. In the first lively second (a second that many cosmologists will devote lifetimes to shaving into ever-finer wafers) are produced gravity and the other forces that govern physics. In less than a minute the universe is a million billion miles across and growing fast. There is a lot of heat now, 10 billion degrees of it, enough to begin the nuclear reactions that create the lighter elements – principally hydrogen and helium, with a dash (about one atom in a hundred million) of lithium. In three minutes 98 percent of all the matter there is or will ever be has been produced. We have a universe. It is a place of the most wondrous and gratifying possibility, and beautiful, too. And it was all done in about the time it takes to make a sandwich.[4]

We take the story further, this time guided by a physicist, the late Sir John Houghton:[5]

It takes about a million years for the universe to cool enough for electrons to attach themselves to the nuclei to form atoms . . . Imagine a region of higher density than the rest. The force of gravity will attract more matter into this more dense region . . . Over a period of millions of years these high-density blobs will become stars and groups of stars will become galaxies . . . Even more extreme conditions are generated as some stars towards the end of their lives blow themselves apart in events known as supernovae . . . It is in these gigantic explosions that heavy elements such as platinum, gold, uranium and a host of others are formed.

This exploded material contains . . . all ninety-two naturally occurring elements of the periodic table. In its turn it mixes with hydrogen and helium gas from the interstellar medium, to go again through the stellar evolutionary process. Second-generation stars are born . . . We believe our sun to be such a second-generation star. Around our sun, planets have formed, probably as gas-and-dust clouds surrounding the young sun gradually fused together into a number of dense objects. Planet earth was born 4.5 thousand million years ago with its rich chemical composition and conditions suitable for the development of life.[6]

Houghton deduced:

For human beings to exist, it can be argued that the whole universe is needed. It needs to be old enough (and therefore large enough) for one generation of stars to have evolved and died, to produce the heavy elements, and then for there to be enough time for a second-generation star like our sun to form with its system of planets. Finally there have to be the right conditions on earth for life to develop, survive and flourish . . . But that is not all. Our current understanding is that for the universe to develop in the right way, incredibly precise fine-tuning[7] has been required in its basic structure and in the conditions at the time of the Big Bang.[8]

Now the idea of a "big bang" is a point of concern for some people who have been influenced by Richard Dawkins's simplistic insistence on our choosing either science or God. However, these are false alternatives, on the same foolish level as insisting that we choose between Henry Ford and a car production line to explain the origin of a Ford Galaxy.[9]

The fact is that both of these explanations are necessary; they do not contradict but rather complement each other. Henry Ford is the agent who designed the car; the car production line is the mechanism by which it is manufactured. Similarly, we do not have to choose between God and the big bang. They are different kinds of explanation – one in terms of God's creatorial agency and the other in terms of mechanism and laws. It is worth pointing out that the Belgian Jesuit priest and cosmologist Georges Lemaître who first suggested a big bang origin also did not think we had to choose between science and religion.[10]

Furthermore, the term "big bang" is essentially a label put on a (fascinating) mystery by Sir Fred Hoyle who, incidentally, did not believe in it. It is used by scientists to express their belief that the universe – more accurately, space-time – had a beginning. Arno Penzias, who won the Nobel Prize for Physics for discovering an echo of that beginning in the cosmic microwave background, wrote: "The best data we have [about whether the universe is open or closed] are exactly what I would have predicted, had I nothing to go on but the five books of Moses, the Psalms and the Bible as a whole."[11] Therefore, the standard (big bang) model developed by physicists and cosmologists can be seen as a scientific unpacking of the implications of the statement, "In the beginning, God created the heavens and the earth."[12] There is a certain irony here, in that the very same big bang cosmological model of the universe that confirms the biblical claim that there was a beginning also implies that the universe is very old.

It is worth reminding ourselves that scientific confirmation of the initial creation event is the kind of thing that the apostle Paul would lead us to expect (Romans 1:19–20). God has left his fingerprints in creation, and so natural theology is a legitimate exercise. That is why I have drawn attention to the current convergence between science and the biblical record on the beginning of space-time.

NOTES

1. One notable such scientist was John Maddox, editor at the time of the scholarly journal *Nature*.

2. Leon Kass, *The Beginning of Wisdom* (Chicago: University of Chicago Press, 2006), 28 n. 4, italics in original.

3. C. John Collins, *Genesis 1–4* (Phillipsburg, NJ: P&R, 2006), 51.

4. Bill Bryson, *A Short History of Nearly Everything* (New York: Broadway, 2004), 10.

5. Former professor of physics at Oxford, then head of the UK Meteorological Office, and subsequently chairman of the Nobel Prize–winning Intergovernmental Panel on Climate Change (IPCC).

6. John Houghton, *The Search for God: Can Science Help?* (Oxford: Lion, 1995), 27–28.

7. For examples of this fine-tuning, see John C. Lennox, *Cosmic Chemistry: Do God and Science Mix?* (Oxford: Lion Hudson, 2021), chapter 7.

8. Houghton, *Search for God*, 33–34.

9. For more detailed explanation, see Lennox, *Cosmic Chemistry*, part 2.

10. See Pablo de Felipe, "Georges Lemaître, the Scientist and Priest Who 'Could Conceive the Beginning of the Universe,'" *BioLogos*, August 23, 2017, https://biologos.org/articles/georges-lemaitre-the-scientist-and-priest-who-could-conceive-the-beginning-of-the-universe.

11. Quoted in Malcolm W. Browne, "Clues to Universe Origin Expected," *New York Times*, March 12, 1978, www.nytimes.com/1978/03/12/archives/clues-to-universe-origin-expected-the-making-of-the-universe.html.

12. Concerning "the heavens and the earth," see chapter 5, endnote 2, p. 157.

APPENDIX C

TWO ACCOUNTS OF CREATION?

An argument frequently advanced against allowing a significant chronological dimension in the early chapters of Genesis is that the creation account given in Genesis 2 contradicts any chronology based on Genesis 1. One point at issue is that chapter 1 describes the creation of the plants before that of humans, whereas Genesis 2 seems to give the reverse impression. Here is the relevant text from Genesis 2:

> When no bush of the field was yet in the land and no small plant of the field had yet sprung up – for the LORD God had not caused it to rain on the land, and there was no man to work the ground, and a mist was going up from the land and was watering the whole face of the ground – then the LORD God formed the man of dust from the ground and breathed into his nostrils the breath of life, and the man became a living creature.

> And the LORD God planted a garden in Eden, in the
> east, and there he put the man whom he had formed.
> And out of the ground the LORD God made to spring
> up every tree that is pleasant to the sight and good for
> food.
>
> *Genesis 2:5–9*

C. John Collins points out that the ESV rendering here of the Hebrew *ha'arets* as "land" rather than "earth" in the first of these verses is preferable, since the lack of plants here is not attributed to the fact that they had not yet been created, but to the fact that there was no rain. In light of that, Collins deduces that the scenario depicted here would be a very familiar one to the readers. They would understand "a land in which the rain falls during the winter and not at all during the summer. This weather pattern makes the ground quite dry and brown by the end of the summer and the coming of the rains brings about plant growth. The only way to overcome this natural pattern is for man to work the ground, by irrigation in this case."[1]

In other words, Collins suggests that the Genesis 2 account has nothing to do with the original creation of plant life on day 3, but rather he is saying that at a particular time of the yearly cycle in a particular land, before the plants had started to grow, God created human beings.[2] Now, this reading of the text clearly assumes that the cycle of nature has been established long enough for it to be relevant, so that in order to harmonize it with the events of day 6, one must conclude, as Collins points out, either that the creation days of Genesis 1 are not (all) ordinary, or that they are separated in time. He regards the first of these two options as preferable, viewing the days as God's workdays, so that how long they are does not affect the act of communication.

In chapter 3 of this book I advance some arguments for the second option, or a variant of it, although it is clear that the effective difference between the two is small. It should be pointed out that the text says: "This is the history of the heavens and the earth [*erets*] when they were created, in the day that the Lord made the earth [*erets*] and the heavens, before any plant of the field was in the earth [*erets*]." The term *erets* can of course mean "the land," but Collins's interpretation requires us to believe that when exactly the same Hebrew term is used three times in one sentence, the third of these means something entirely different from the first two, and that the original hearers would immediately pick up on this. The earlier different uses of *erets* in Genesis 1 (heaven and earth and calling the dry land earth) indicate to anyone that this must be a new use of the term, but there is no such contextual indication here.

Another suggestion that has been made is that the order in the first creation account is principally chronological, whereas in the second it is principally logical. Indeed, in ordinary speech and writing, we often mix logical order with chronological order without necessarily being aware of it. Jim bought a car. He drove it home. You ask where he keeps it. Well, he built a garage to put it in. He built the garage when he brought it home? No, the garage was actually already there. That fact could have been made clearer in English by using the pluperfect tense "he had built" rather than using the simple past tense "he built."

Hebrew does not have a separate pluperfect tense, with the result that precise chronological sequence is not always as immediately clear in Hebrew as it could be in English. For this reason, some argue that the order of events in Genesis 2:5–9 clashes with that in Genesis 1 only if we assume that both orders are of the same type. However, the matter is resolved if the first account is predominantly chronological, describing the sweep of creation from its beginning to its goal, the creation of human beings, whereas the second account places man at the center and gives a predominantly logical account of what it means to be human, a circumstance that not all translations make clear.[3]

However, Hebrew has ways of expressing a pluperfect sense that help to solve another apparent chronological clash between Genesis 1 and 2. Some translations of Genesis 2:19 suggest that the creation of animals took place after that of man. For example, "Out of the ground the LORD God formed every beast of the field and every bird of the sky, and brought them to the man to see what he would call them" (NASB). Collins argues that the Hebrew verb should be translated by the pluperfect "had formed" (ESV, NIV, for example), thus obviating the chronological clash.[4] However, the Septuagint does not make the distinction in Greek, which does have a pluperfect tense.

NOTES

1. C. John Collins, *Genesis 1–4* (Phillipsburg, NJ: P&R, 2006), 126.

2. A (major) variant of this view is that of John Sailhamer, *Genesis Unbound: A Provocative New Look at the Creation Account* (Sisters, OR: Multnomah, 1996). He holds that Genesis 1:1 describes the period of the creation of the universe and Genesis 1:2–2:4a describes a one-week period (in the usual sense) during which a particular land, the promised land, was prepared and human beings created in it.

3. The NIV uses the pluperfect English tense to bring out the sense that maintains the chronology. For more detailed comments on the use of the pluperfect, see Alistair McKitterick, "The Language of Genesis," in *Should Christians Embrace Evolution? Biblical and Scientific Responses*, ed. Norman C. Nevin (Nottingham, UK: Inter-Varsity, 2009), and the references given there. However, it should be noted that Robert Gordon holds that introducing the pluperfect only gives partial and superficial relief to the perceived tension between the narratives of Genesis 1 and Genesis 2 (see "The Week That Made the World: Reflections on the First Pages of the Bible," in *Reading the Law: Studies in Honour of Gordon J. Wenham*, ed. J. G. McConville and Karl Moeller [London: T&T Clark, 2007]).

4. C. John Collins, "The *Wayyiqtol* as 'Pluperfect': When and Why?" *Tyndale Bulletin* 46, no. 1 (1995): 117–40, https://legacy.tyndalehouse.com/tynbul/Library/TynBull_1995_46_1_08_Collins_WAYYIQTOL_Pluperfect.pdf.

THEISTIC EVOLUTION AND THE GOD OF THE GAPS

According to Genesis 1 the sequence of creation acts came to an end. On the seventh day God rested. The work of creation was done. That would seem to imply that what went on during the creation sequence is no longer happening, an implication that has consequences for one of the major assumptions of science – the uniformity of nature, the idea that the present holds the key to the past, at least to within a minute fraction of a second from the beginning.

Putting it another way, Genesis seems to suggest that nature has not been absolutely uniform. It is not denying the important fact that nature is *largely* uniform. Indeed, a further implication of the Sabbath is that, after his creation activity, God continues to sustain the universe. The universe constantly depends on his providential care,[1] which means we can rely on the regularities of nature that God himself built in at the beginning. A famous example of this is contained in a statement of Jesus: "For he makes his sun rise on the evil and on the good, and sends rain on the just and on the unjust" (Matthew 5:45). Christianity, therefore, is not to be equated with deism, which holds that God lit the fuse triggering the origin of the universe and then retired from the scene and had no further involvement. The very concept of the Sabbath implies that God's providence in maintaining the universe in existence does not exhaust what the Bible means by *creation*.

The New Testament confirms these two aspects of God's relationship to the universe as both Creator and Sustainer. Paul ascribes these two functions to Christ: "For by him all things were created"; and "In him all things hold together" (Colossians 1:16, 17). Similarly, the letter to the Hebrews says of Christ, "through whom also he created the world"; and "he upholds the universe by the word of his power" (Hebrews 1:2, 3).

According to Genesis, then, creation arguably involved not just one but a sequence of several discrete creation acts,[2] after which God rested. This surely implies that those acts may well have involved processes that are not going on at the moment. Of course, such (supernatural) creation acts ("from above") would appear to science ("from below") as discontinuities or singularities, a suggestion that is highly unpalatable to scientists in general and biologists in particular – especially, but not only, if they are atheists.

For example, physicist Paul Davies, whom I referred to earlier,[3] writes (from a nontheistic perspective):

Ascribing the origin of life to a divine miracle not only is anathema to scientists but also is theologically suspect. The term "God of the gaps" was coined to deride the notion that God can be invoked as an explanation whenever scientists have gaps in their understanding. The trouble with invoking God in this way is that, as science advances, the gaps close, and God gets progressively squeezed out of the story of nature. Theologians long ago accepted that they would forever be fighting a rearguard battle if they tried to challenge science on its own ground. Using the formation of life to prove the existence of God is a tactic that risks instant demolition should someone succeed in making life in a test tube.[4] And the idea that God acts in fits and starts, moving atoms around on odd occasions in competition with natural forces, is a decidedly uninspiring image of the Grand Architect.[5]

Many scientists who believe in God think, similarly, that the idea of God interfering or, less pejoratively, intervening at intervals is a kind of semi-deism and is unworthy of God. They hold that nature possesses "functional integrity," in the sense that life is the fruitful outworking, according to the God-given laws of nature, of the potential built into the capabilities of matter by God at the beginning without a need for further discrete intervention. Surely a theistic evolution[6] of this kind, they say, is more worthy of God than millions of different supernatural acts of creation to produce the vast array of species – even though there is no suggestion (in Genesis or by me) that there were millions of separate creation acts. After all, the number of occurrences of the phrase "And God said . . ." is very small.[7]

This brings us to the issue of interpretations of early Genesis after Darwin. Rabbi Jonathan Sacks says that Jewish interpreters have tended to be comfortable with the idea of evolution:

> The idea that evolution shows that life emerged by chance does not impress the religious mind, which knows from many biblical examples that what appears to be random is in fact providential. The book of Esther, like the story of Joseph, is a providential narrative in which everything happens at the right time in the right way to bring about the fated end, yet the word "God" does not appear in the book, and the festival to which it gave rise, Purim, means "lotteries" or chance. In general, what appears to human eyes as chance is seen through the eyes of faith to be divinely intended. "When the lot is cast in the lap, its entire verdict has been decided by God" (Proverbs 16:33).[8]

Sacks cites Rabbi J. H. Hertz (1872–1946) to the effect that "'there is nothing inherently un-Jewish in the evolutionary conception of the origin and growth of forms of existence from the simple to the complex, and from the lowest to the highest,' provided we acknowledge that '*each stage is no product of chance, but is an act of Divine will*, realising the divine purpose, and receiving the seal of the divine approval.'"[9]

This view is echoed in the present day by eminent biologist and Christian, Francis Collins, director of the National Institutes of Health in the United States and the winner of the 2020 Templeton Prize, who says: "Evolution could appear to us to be driven by chance, but from God's perspective the outcome would be entirely specified. Thus God could be completely and intimately involved in the creation of all species, while from our perspective, limited as it is by the tyranny of linear time, this would appear a random and undirected process."[10]

Theistic evolution was the view championed by Asa Gray, considered to be the most important American botanist of the nineteenth century, who was Charles Darwin's chief supporter on that continent. Gray was a Christian, as was Theodosius Dobzhansky (1900–1975), a Ukrainian-American geneticist regarded as one of the main architects of evolutionary theory. In 1996 Pope John Paul II cleared the way for the Roman Catholic Church to approve evolution by his announcement at the Pontifical Academy of Sciences in Rome that "new findings lead us toward the recognition of evolution as more than a hypothesis." However, he was careful to add: "If the origin of the human body comes through living matter which existed previously, the spiritual soul is created directly by God."[11]

Francis Collins describes his understanding of theistic evolution as follows:

I found this elegant evidence of the relatedness of all living things an occasion of awe, and came to see this as the master plan of the same Almighty who caused the universe to come into being and set its physical parameters just precisely right to allow the creation of stars, planets, heavy elements, and life itself. Without knowing its name at the time, I settled comfortably into a synthesis generally referred to as "theistic evolution," a position I find enormously satisfying to this day.[12]

Collins goes on to flesh out his position:

God, who is not limited in space and time, created the universe and established natural laws that govern it. Seeking to populate this otherwise sterile universe with living creatures, God chose the elegant mechanism of evolution to create microbes, plants, and animals of all sorts. Most remarkably, God intentionally chose the same mechanism to give rise to special creatures who would have intelligence, a knowledge of right and wrong, free will and a desire to seek fellowship with Him.[13]

However, Collins explains, there came a point in history when God specially conferred his image on a creature that had emerged from the evolutionary process. This was the beginning of the human race "made in the image of God."[14]

The main points of this version of theistic evolution are:

1. God causes the universe to come into being.
2. God sets the laws of physics and the fine-tuned initial conditions.
3. God sustains the universe in being.
4. The universe develops and life subsequently emerges, without any more special discrete supernatural input from God until God creates human beings.
5. At a particular moment, God specially conferred his image on a hominid that had already emerged from the gradual evolutionary process.[15]

There are other versions of theistic evolution. For instance, one variant denies point 5, claiming that point 4 includes the emergence of human beings. Biochemist and intelligent design proponent Michael Behe accepts 1, 2, and 3, but not 4. He believes that evolution has occurred in the Darwinian sense, but that it has been "supervised." He argues that the scientific picture is that natural selection and *random* mutation do something, but that their reach is relatively limited: there is an "edge" or limit to evolution's variational capacity that can be transcended only if mutations are introduced that are *nonrandom*. In other words, Behe is suggesting that an input of intelligence is needed and that a designer[16] got involved in these mutations. Thus, on this view, God moved atoms on many occasions in the evolutionary process. However, Behe, and other ID people, does not believe that design *only* occurs where there are gaps in the causal sequences. His point is that only at these points can we *prove* there is design. He does not believe that God is only in the gaps.

The C. S. Lewis/Francis Collins version of theistic evolution as it applies to the origin of human beings also involves moving atoms, since it is very hard to imagine, granted our current insights into the brain and its functioning, how God could impart his image to a pre-existing creature without fundamental adjustments to the neural system in the brain to create the necessary physical substrate to carry this new dimension of God-consciousness.

Cambridge paleobiologist Simon Conway Morris gives a further variant of theistic evolution. He suggests that the uncanny ability of evolution to find its way through the space of all possible paths to what he calls "life's solution" is congruent with creation: "For some it will remain as the pointless activity of the Blind Watchmaker, but others may prefer to remove their dark glasses. The choice, of course, is yours."[17]

Now all of this has the salutary effect of forcing me to think very hard. First of all, I am not a biologist (though I try hard to understand what biologists write), and secondly, and more importantly, I have the greatest respect and admiration for these people and their stand against atheism. In particular, Francis Collins has been a great encouragement to me personally over the years. However, even though the dominant position among biologists who are Christian is theistic evolution, I still wish to add my pennyworth to the discussion.

As a scientist I am sensitive to the danger of falling into a "God of the gaps" mentality and running the risk of intellectual laziness. For that reason I hasten to say that I do not find the main evidence for God's activity in the current gaps in the scientific picture. I see evidence of God everywhere in the science we do know – indeed, I see it in the very fact that we can do science. I agree wholeheartedly with Francis Collins that God created the natural laws that govern the universe. God is the God of the whole show. Indeed, for me as a mathematician the very mathematical intelligibility of the universe, and the subtlety and power of the mathematics developed to describe it, constitutes major evidence for the existence of a Creator.

I go further. I also agree that God is the cause of the universe's coming into being and continued existence, and that God fine-tuned its physical parameters and set its initial boundary conditions so that the formation of the elements and (at least two[18]) generations of stars occurred that ultimately gave rise to planets endowed with the heavy elements that are necessary for life. The supremely important issue is that God did it – not how he did it, a secondary issue over which we may well have differences of opinion.

At that level, where I begin to have problems with theistic evolution[19] is at the next stage. So far we have been thinking not about biology but about cosmology, physics, and chemistry. As a result of a process inaugurated and supervised by God and covered by the known laws of physics, which were designed by God, we have arrived at a world that possesses the raw materials of life.

Theistic evolution now asks why we should introduce a *special* supernatural act of creation at the point of the origin of life. Would it not be more consistent, it says, to think that the origin and development of life proceeded in exactly the same way as the processes before the origin of life? Surely it would be a pity, having come so far, now to introduce a God (of the gaps) simply because there is, as yet, no plausible explanation for the origin of life, wouldn't it? This last point is rather ironic, because by it theistic evolutionists open themselves up to the very same charge over the origin of the universe and, in many cases, the origin of human life.

Of course, the issue is not whether or not God could have done it in a particular way. Clearly, as a basic principle, God, being God, can do it any way he chooses. I agree with Francis Collins on that point as well. The most important thing by far is that *God did it*. And God has, so far as we can see, chosen to do *part* of it by secondary causation – what we often call "natural processes," like the formation of galaxies, suns, and planets under gravity and other forces of nature without constant divine intervention. The question is, did God do it *all* in that way? Is there any reason to think that there were several discrete acts of creation (for example, origin of life, humans) within the history of the universe that are fundamentally different from events that normally happen in God's world governed by his laws?

And why does it matter anyway? Is this not a case of Christians getting involved in an irrelevant sideshow? I do not think so, especially in light of the current insistence on the part of many atheists that there is nothing special about human beings, since they have been produced by precisely the same blind and unguided process as any other species. The status of human beings is no small matter.

SINGULARITIES, MIRACLES, AND THE SUPERNATURAL

Three considerations weigh with me at this juncture. Firstly, it is common knowledge that most physicists seem to be comfortable with the view that the origin of space-time is a singularity beyond the reach of science. Certainly, theistic evolutionists also seem comfortable with the idea that God was responsible for that singularity as Creator – he was the First Cause. The universe did not come to be through natural processes. The reason something exists rather than nothing is that God willed it to be so.

Secondly, as we pointed out earlier, many theistic evolutionists hold that the origin of human life involved some kind of supernatural discontinuity.

Thirdly, and most importantly, it is part of the historic Christian faith that there have been other singularities in more recent history – pre-eminently the incarnation and resurrection of Jesus Christ. These events have a physical dimension, but they clearly do not fall within the range of the explanatory power of the laws of nature. On the contrary, these events were caused, as the New Testament indicates, by the direct input of divine power from outside.

Yet those of us who are Christians believe that these events actually occurred, even though many of our atheist scientific colleagues protest that the laws of nature forbid such occurrences.[20]

That being the case, I find it strange that some Christians seem to find a priori difficulty in the claim that there have been some additional singularities in the past, like the origin of life and the origin of human beings. Surely if one grants, say, at least three major singularities – creation, the incarnation, and the resurrection – there can be no in-principle objection to believing in (a relatively few) more singularities, especially if there is both scientific and biblical evidence to support them. Not only that, but Charles Darwin's contemporary Alfred Russel Wallace also thought there were discontinuities at the origin of life – the origin of consciousness and the origin of specifically human faculties. Wallace has been called the forgotten man of evolution, as he had worked out the theory of natural selection and sent his idea to Charles Darwin. Wallace deserved priority and much more credit than he ever received until relatively recently.

The question now arises whether we are to think of the singularities involved in creation as miracles. For instance, biologist Denis Alexander writes:

> In biblical thought the language of miracles seems to be generally reserved for those special and unusual workings of God in his *created order* and in the lives of his people. This does not exclude the possibility that

God performs particular miracles during the *work of creation*, but if that is the case then Scripture is silent about that aspect of his *creative work*. When Jesus intervenes to turn water into wine, or calm a rough sea, or raise Lazarus from the dead, these miraculous signs stand out as such because they are so different from God's normal way of working in *creation*.

Science is based on observed regularities and logical induction to unobserved regularities. The secular scientist assumes that everything works in a regular, reproducible kind of way because that is what science has always found to be the case so far. The scientist who is a Christian agrees, but in addition believes in a logical basis for that order, the *creator* God who faithfully endows the universe with its regularities and intelligibility.

There is something paradoxical about the suggestion that miracles can be regular or even predictable events in God's *general work of creation*. The whole point about miracles is that they are unexpected, irregular events, particular signs of God's grace, so my suggestion is that Christians use the language of miracle with this biblical understanding in mind.[21]

We note that Alexander uses the word *creation* both to describe the original act of creation at which God endowed the universe with its regularities and to describe the product of that act – the creation that now exists and whose regularities are studied by scientists. These regularities are understood to be part of what Alexander calls "God's general work of creation," presumably referring to God's continuing to hold the universe with its regularities in existence – the "present tense" of creation, as he calls it.[22] These are distinctions I readily accept, if I have understood him correctly.

For us to be able to recognize "miracle" in the New Testament sense of "wonder" or "sign," as C. S. Lewis pointed out, the universe must exhibit regularities that are known. Otherwise, as Alexander says, Jesus' miracles would not "stand out." However, such miracles, as Lewis went on to argue, do not "break" the regularities enshrined in the laws of nature. It is rather that God (the Lawgiver) feeds a new event into the system by his divine power. It is an exceptional, as distinct from a normal, act of God.[23]

Since the miracles of the Bible are recognized as such because they stand out against the known regularities of the universe, the term *miracle* would scarcely be strictly appropriate for the initial creation of the universe with those regularities. However, this does not mean that the initial creation did not involve a number of direct interventions by God in order to *set up* the universe with its regularities. The word *supernatural* would therefore be more appropriate. Denis Alexander seems to miss this distinction. After all, the statement "In the beginning was the Word . . . All things were made through him" (John 1:1, 3) does not use the language of miracle, although supernatural activity of the highest order was clearly involved.

It follows that, although the word *miracle* is not used, the Bible is not silent on the fact that God's *supernatural* activity was involved at creation. Indeed, that seems to be the whole point of the creation sequence – to differentiate, *within* the period from the absolute beginning to the flowering of human civilization, between God's special creation acts and his providence (or "general work of creation," to use Alexander's phrase) in holding the universe in being in the intervals between those acts and subsequently.

It is failure to distinguish the miraculous from the supernatural that led Alexander to make what seems to be a very strange statement: "There is something paradoxical about the suggestion that miracles can be regular or even predictable events in God's general work of creation." No one, as far as I am aware, would think of saying that miracles are regular or predictable events.[24] What I am suggesting is that both the direct supernatural action of God and his providence were involved during the creation period.[25]

Finally, I think that Alexander's tautologous assertion that science has so far *always* found that *everything* works in a regular, reproducible kind of way is untenable.[26]

In theological terms, theistic evolution adopts an essentially Augustinian view of creation as ultimate causation. That is, *creation* expresses the idea of the dependency of the universe on God: God causes the universe and its laws to exist and endows it with its potential.[27] Such dependency is, of course, a fundamental aspect of creation, but I do not think this is all that is implied by the biblical use of the term *creation*. For in both the Old and New Testaments, the Bible clearly distinguishes between God's initial acts of creation, on the one hand, and his subsequent upholding of the universe, on the other. This distinction is also apparent in Genesis 1: it records a sequence of creation acts followed by God's resting. I also think, in contrast with my theistic evolutionary friends, that science supports this distinction.

ARE ALL GAPS BAD?

That brings us back to the matter of gaps. There would appear to be different kinds of gaps, as I have argued in detail elsewhere.[28] Some gaps are gaps of ignorance and are eventually closed by increased scientific knowledge; they are the bad gaps that figure in the expression "God of the gaps." But there are other gaps – gaps that are *revealed* by advancing science (good gaps). The fact that the information on a printed page is not within the explanatory power of physics and chemistry is not a gap of ignorance; it is a gap that has to do with the nature of writing, and we know how to fill it – namely, with the input of intelligence.

As we have seen – so forgive me if I labour the point – physicists and cosmologists have become accustomed to the idea that their mathematical model of the origin and expansion of space-time leads them to conclude that there is a singularity or gap at that origin where the laws of physics break down. Most Christians readily accept that the ultimate explanation of that singularity, and of the laws of nature, is God. That means they accept that, although God can act indirectly, there must be some point or points at which he acts directly. Causing the universe to exist in the first place was surely one such direct action of God.[29]

In this connection, one of the things I find striking is that, after stating that God created the heavens and the earth,[30] the creation narrative, as I understand it, passes over vast stretches of time (and much physical and chemical activity) with no comment whatsoever until we arrive at a formless and empty earth. It is at that point that Genesis 1:2 tells us, "The Spirit of God was hovering over the face of the waters."

Astrophysicist Hugh Ross suggests that this statement gives us a frame of reference and point of view just above the surface of the earth in a specific place.[31] This, incidentally, may well provide an answer to the question: If most of Genesis 1 is concerned with global phenomena – the heavens, earth, land, sea, sky, and so on – why does it talk about day and night, even though night and day occur simultaneously on different sides of the earth?[32]

More than that, reference to the Spirit of God hovering near earth could be understood as a dramatic indication not only *that* God's special action is now going to begin but *where* it is going to begin. The aeons of waiting are over. The Creator is about to shape his world, to create life and fill the earth with it in preparation for God's crowning final act, the making of man and woman in his image.

That impression of special action is strongly confirmed

in the biblical account of the origin of life. We are told that God spoke on day three more than once. Firstly, God separates the dry land and the sea. Then God speaks again: "And God said, 'Let the earth sprout vegetation'" (Genesis 1:11). In other words, as I said earlier, according to Genesis, you do not get from inorganic matter to organic by unguided natural processes.[33] Life does not emerge from nonlife without God having to get directly involved and speak his word.[34]

The question is, does science give any evidence for such singularities? My answer is that just as science and the Bible converge and complement each other on the origin of the universe, so do they on the origin of life.

Firstly, we must clear away a major potential misunderstanding briefly mentioned above. Contrary to widespread public impression, (neo-)Darwinian evolution cannot account for the *origin* of life. Richard Dawkins was simply wrong when he said in *The Blind Watchmaker* that natural selection explained not only the variation in life but also the *existence* of life.[35] His error has nothing to do with belief in God but is a simple matter of logic. Darwinian evolution *presupposes* the existence of a mutating replicator in order to get going in the first place. Hence Darwinian evolution cannot be an explanation for the *existence* of the very thing without which it itself cannot get started. This obvious fact was recognized long ago by the famous Russian biologist Theodosius Dobzhansky, who said, "Prebiological natural selection is a contradiction in terms."[36]

It is good to see that in his book *The Greatest Show on Earth*,[37] Dawkins admits that natural selection cannot explain the existence of life. However, he goes on to say something very odd: "We don't actually need a plausible theory of the origin of life, and we might even be a little bit anxious if a too plausible theory were to be discovered!" His argument is that if there were a plausible theory, then life should be common in the galaxy. But what has the commonness of life in the galaxy to do with the *plausibility* of a theory of life's origin? A plausible theory might well confine the likelihood of life existing to earth. In fact, a plausible theory of the origin of life does exist – namely, that God created it on a planet he had specially prepared for that purpose.

What Dawkins may mean is that if there were a plausible *naturalistic* theory showing that where the physical and chemical conditions were such and such, life was more or less bound to occur, then we would, on statistical grounds, expect there to be quite a lot of life out there. But there isn't such a theory, and recent research gives little hope of one. This last point is important, since the evolutionary theory that is normally subsumed under theistic evolution is neo-Darwinism. However, that theory is now regarded by an increasing number of biologists, including systems biologists Denis Noble at the University of Oxford and James Shapiro at the University of Chicago, as inadequate. They think that it needs not only revision but replacement by something much more sophisticated. Clearly this has implications for the *scientific* soundness of adopting what might be called a theistic neo-Darwinism – if that does not sound too self-contradictory.[38]

A MATTER OF INFORMATION

The catch is that the nature of life itself strongly militates against there ever being a purely *naturalistic* theory of life's origin. There is an immense gulf between the nonliving and the living that is a matter of kind, not simply of degree. It is like the gulf between the raw materials paper and ink, on the one hand, and the finished product of paper with writing on it, on the other. Raw materials do not self-organize into linguistic structures. Such structures are not "emergent" phenomena, in the sense that they do not appear without intelligent input.

Any adequate explanation for the existence of the DNA-coded database and for the prodigious information storage and processing capabilities of the living cell must involve a source of information that transcends the basic physical and chemical materials out of which the cell is constructed. As Microsoft founder Bill Gates once put it: "Human DNA is like a computer program, but far, far more advanced than any software we've ever created."[39] Such processors and programs, on the basis of all we know from computer science, cannot be explained, even in principle, without the involvement of a mind.

Amir Aczel, a mathematician, writes: "Having seen how DNA stores and manipulates tremendous amounts of information . . . and uses the information to control life, we are left with one big question: What created DNA . . . Was it perhaps the power, thinking, and will of a supreme being that created this self-replicating basis of all life?"[40] The answer is surely yes.

Unguided natural processes do not generate the language-type information found in RNA and DNA.[41] Indeed, even if unguided natural processes were to produce a machine (which assumption is, of course, essential to atheistic belief), that machine still would not create any novel information. Leon Brillouin, in his classic work on information theory, writes: "A machine does not create any new information, but it performs a very valuable transformation of known information."[42]

What I find odd about the (theistic) evolutionary view of the origin of life is that it seems to fly in the face of these scientific considerations. I fail to see evidence that the God-given laws of nature, working on the matter he created, starting with initial conditions set by him, are adequate to ensure that the universe and life will "emerge" without any special, discrete, supernatural input. Mathematical laws of the type that are familiar to us from physics are just not adequate to do the job, for the simple reason that they cannot create information – as is recognized by some leading physicists.

For instance, Paul Davies asks: "Can *specific randomness* be the guaranteed product of a deterministic, mechanical, lawlike process, like a primordial soup left to the mercy of familiar laws of physics and chemistry? No, it couldn't. No known law could achieve this – a fact of the deepest significance."[43]

And yet the claim is that such processes not only created information but also created a creature that could create information. Surely not! Scientific considerations from information theory point in the exact opposite direction, straight towards a special, intelligent, creative act as the only credible solution to the question of the origin of life's biological information.[44]

This contrasts sharply with a remark made by Denis Alexander on the origin of life: "Imagine going into an artist's studio . . . and then telling the artist, 'You've chosen the wrong type of paints, they're really hopeless!' I think we would all agree that would be insulting. But to confidently proclaim that the precious materials God has so carefully brought into being in the dying moments of exploding stars do not have the potentiality to bring about life seems to me equally insulting."[45]

This argument is fatally flawed, since the analogy does not correspond to the application. No one is suggesting that the Creator's materials are "the wrong type" or "hopeless." What is being suggested is that the Creator's good materials cannot bring life into existence without the additional direct intelligent input of the Creator. This is no more an insult to the Creator than it would be an insult to the artist to suggest that his paints are incapable of producing a masterpiece without his direct input. It is rather the (ludicrous) suggestion that the paints could do it on their own without him that would be an insult to the painter!

Furthermore, it is no more intellectual laziness to reject the idea that life is a product of the latent potential of matter and energy working according to the laws of nature than it is intellectual laziness to abandon the search for perpetual motion, or to attribute a magnificent painting to the creative genius of Leonardo da Vinci rather than to the latent physical and chemical capacities of paint and canvas.

And that brings us back to Paul Davies's assertion that "the idea that God acts in fits and starts, moving atoms around on odd occasions in competition with natural forces, is a decidedly uninspiring image of the Grand Architect."[46] Firstly, the idea that the God who invented natural forces could be in competition with them sounds self-contradictory. What, then, about the business of God moving atoms? Leonardo da Vinci can also help us here. Neither the mind nor information is a material substance. Yet the conceptual information in Leonardo's mind moved the atoms in his hand that moved the atoms of the paintbrush that moved the atoms of paint that produced his masterpieces. None of those movements were in *competition* with natural forces. On the contrary, they *involved* natural forces directed by mind. God is Spirit, and not material. And since God moved atoms (or rather created them) to launch the universe, since he moved atoms to raise Jesus from the dead, it follows that Davies has got it completely wrong. It would be an "uninspiring image" of the Creator *not* to credit him with moving atoms at the origin of life and at the creation of his masterpiece – human beings made in his image in such a way that their minds could move atoms too.

COMMON ANCESTRY?

The idea of a special creation of human beings will be challenged by the following evolutionary argument. Human beings and animals share many common features in terms of large-scale structures of bones and organs, down to the similarities in their genetic material. These features imply that there is a seamless evolution by natural unguided processes, up through the forms of life from primitive to complex. Although there are gaps in the fossil record, there is nevertheless a fairly universal consensus among biologists that the details will eventually be filled in. They regard the molecular evidence for the evolutionary interrelatedness of all life to be essentially conclusive.

The similarities are undeniable. But similarities can be a result of design as distinct from descent, or, indeed, of a combination of the two, as selective breeding demonstrates. Therefore, a naturalistic explanation of the similarities in terms of natural selection carries authority only in so far as there is evidence that the suggested mechanisms can bear the weight that is put on them. As I argue in detail elsewhere,[47] they clearly can bear some weight – indeed, variation involving natural selection and mutation can be observed and is noncontroversial. However, whether or not they can bear the weight of the difference between animals and humans is another matter. And it is a quantum difference. Geneticist Steve Jones writes:

> A chimp may share ninety-eight percent of its genes with a typical human being but it is certainly not ninety-eight percent human: it is not human at all – it is a chimp. And does the fact that we have genes in common with a mouse, or a banana, say anything new about human nature? There have been claims that scientists will soon find the gene that makes us human. The ancestral message will then at last allow us to understand what we really are. The idea seems to me ridiculous.[48]

In his book *The Music of Life*, Denis Noble, a pioneer systems biologist, explains in more detail how tiny differences in genome sequence can encode enormously complex differences in function. However, Noble also points out about the genome (and indeed the brain) that "we need to recognise that these are databases that the system as a whole uses. They are not programs that determine the behaviour of the system."[49] Intriguingly, Noble likens the human genome, with its roughly thirty thousand genes, to an immense organ with thirty thousand pipes (there are such organs): "The music is an integrated activity of the organ. It is not just a series of notes. But the music itself is not created by the organ. The organ is not a program that writes, for example, the Bach fugues. Bach did that. And it requires an accomplished organist to make the organ perform." Noble then asks: "If there is an organ, and some music, who is the player and who was the composer? And is there a conductor?"[50] Excellent questions. Whether Noble has answered them satisfactorily is another matter, but the very fact that he is asking them is a heartening change from the extreme reductionism that has characterized much of the writing on this issue.

Biologists Jerry Fodor and Massimo Piattelli-Palmarini, though not doubting that evolution has occurred, are deeply concerned about the "distressingly uncritical" nature of "much of the vast neo-Darwinian literature," and concerned that "the methodological skepticism that characterises most areas of scientific discourse seems strikingly absent when Darwinism is the topic." This, according to them, applies particularly to the role played by natural selection.

> Natural selection has shown insidious imperialistic tendencies. The offering of post-hoc explanations of phenotypic traits by reference to their hypothetical effects on fitness in their hypothetical environments of selection has spread from evolutionary theory to a host of other traditional disciplines: philosophy, psychology, anthropology, sociology and even to aesthetics and theology. Some people really do think that natural selection is a universal acid, and that nothing can resist its powers of dissolution.

However, the internal evidence to back this imperialistic selectionism strikes us as very thin. Its credibility depends largely on the reflected glamour of natural selection which biology proper is said to legitimise. Accordingly, if natural selection disappears from biology, its offshoots in other fields seem likely to disappear as well. This is an outcome much to be desired since, more often than not, these offshoots have proved to be not just post hoc but ad hoc, crude, reductionist, scientistic rather than scientific, shamelessly self-congratulatory, and so wanting in detail that they are bound to accommodate the data, however that data may turn out. So it really does matter whether natural selection is true.[51]

In our context, one of the most interesting statements by Jerry Fodor comes in an earlier article:

In fact an appreciable number of perfectly reasonable biologists are coming to think that the theory of natural selection can no longer be taken for granted . . .

The present worry is that the explication of natural selection by appeal to selective breeding is seriously misleading, and that it thoroughly misled Darwin. Because *breeders have minds*, there's a fact of the matter about what traits they breed for; if you want to know, just ask them. Natural selection, by contrast, is mindless; it acts without malice aforethought. That strains the analogy between natural selection and breeding, perhaps to the breaking point. What, then, is the intended interpretation when one speaks of natural selection? The answer is wide open as of this writing.[52]

Unsurprisingly, Fodor has provoked a storm.

And he is not the only one raising questions about natural selection. Biologist William Provine, in a remarkable afterword published in a new edition of a classic work, explains that his views have "changed dramatically":

> Natural selection does not act on anything, nor does it select (for, or against), force, maximize, create, modify, shape, operate, drive, favor, maintain, push, or adjust. Natural selection does nothing. Natural selection as a natural force belongs in the insubstantial category already populated by the Becher/Stahl phlogiston ... or Newton's "ether" ...
>
> Having natural selection select is nifty because it excuses the necessity of talking about the actual causation of natural selection. Such talk was excusable for Charles Darwin, but inexcusable for Darwinists now. Creationists have discovered our empty "natural selection" language, and the "actions" of natural selection make huge, vulnerable targets.[53]

More recently, biologist Robert Reid has added to the question marks over natural selection in his comprehensive work *Biological Emergences*,[54] of which a reviewer, Christopher Rose, wrote: "Reid argues convincingly that the selectionist paradigm is a conceptual dead-end for understanding innovation since it mistakenly views natural selection as a creative force in evolution."[55] Reid is well aware of the risks of his undertaking: "Since neo-Darwinists are also hypersensitive to creationism, they treat any criticism of the current paradigm as a breach of the scientific worldview that will admit the fundamentalist hordes. Consequently, questions about how selection theory can claim to be the all-sufficient explanation of evolution go unanswered or ignored."[56] He then details substantial evidence that natural selection cannot bear the weight that is often put upon it.

It would now seem that Richard Dawkins's concession (of the obvious fact) that natural selection does not account for the origin of life is far from adequate. Natural selection would appear to account for very little at all in the development of life.

This does not, of course, mean that the scientists quoted above have given up on the naturalist paradigm. It does mean, though, that there is a shift away from simplistic reductionism to "emergentist" explanations that raise even more sharply the question of the input of information from an intelligent source and make the a priori exclusion of such input appear all the more arbitrary. For "emergence" is turning out to be another slippery term that can mask a number of hidden assumptions.[57]

Welcoming Reid's book, the reviewer interestingly concludes:

> Whether one is ready to accept a formal theory of emergentism or embrace its dialectical synthesis with selectionism, Reid's championing of emergence is a necessary step in the right direction. On the upside, evolutionary biology needs to be pushed beyond reductionist/gene-centric explanations for properties like multicellularity, body plans, behavioral flexibility, self-maintenance, homology, and human intelligence. The important events in life's history clearly involved causal factors at numerous levels of organization, none of which have inherent priority over the others. On the downside, emergentism will undoubtedly increase the challenges of teaching evolution theory and convincing the public (and ourselves) that biologists know what we are talking about.[58]

There have been major developments in this area since the first edition of *Seven Days That Divide the World* appeared. Denis Noble, mentioned above, is part of a group of scientists called the Third Way who have amassed a great deal of evidence from biology to show that the modern synthesis (neo-Darwinism) needs to be replaced, as it is both outdated and inadequate. This is a very important and indeed fascinating development, and for those readers who wish to pursue it further, I have given detailed attention to it and its implications in my book *Cosmic Chemistry*.[59]

EVOLUTION OF THE GAPS?

Although the charge of believing in a God of the gaps must be taken seriously – it is, after all, possible for a theist to be intellectually lazy and say, in effect, "I can't explain it; therefore God did it" – it is important to say that what's sauce for the goose is sauce for the gander.

Evolution is also a notorious gap-filler. It is not hard to cobble up a speculative, just-so story and say that "evolution did it." Indeed, a scientist of naturalist convictions *has* to say that natural processes were solely responsible for the existence of life and all of its various forms, since there is no admissible alternative in the naturalistic worldview.

Nobel laureate physicist Robert Laughlin, whose research is on the properties of matter that make life possible, issued the following warning to scientists about the dangers of this kind of thinking:

> Much of present-day biological knowledge is ideological. A key symptom of ideological thinking is the explanation that has no implications and cannot be tested. I call such logical dead ends antitheories because they have exactly the opposite effect of real theories: they stop thinking rather than stimulate it. Evolution by natural selection, for instance, which Charles Darwin originally conceived as a great theory, has lately come to function as an antitheory, called upon to cover up embarrassing experimental shortcomings and legitimize

findings that are at best questionable and at worst not even wrong. Your protein defies the laws of mass action? Evolution did it! Your complicated mess of chemical reactions turns into a chicken? Evolution! The human brain works on logical principles no computer can emulate? Evolution is the cause![60]

I suspect that belief in an evolution of the gaps is probably more widespread than belief in a God of the gaps, since concentration on the latter allows the former to thrive undetected.

Tempted as I am to explore this matter further, I must leave it here with a thought experiment about descent and design. Suppose that scientists manage one day to produce life in the laboratory from nonliving chemicals – as many believe they will, in light of Craig Venter's construction of a synthetic bacterium using a genome contained in a computer program. Suppose, further, that this life thrives and establishes itself as a new species – species X, say. Now imagine that all scientific records of this are lost, and in the far-distant future, scientists come across species X. If they still hold to neo-Darwinism, which is now looking less and less likely to be the case, as mentioned above, these scientists would inevitably argue that species X is related to all other life by an uninterrupted naturalistic evolutionary process. They would be wrong, would they not? The relationship of species X to other species involves a special and discrete input of information by intelligence. What is more, that intervention of human intelligence would, by definition, be invisible to naturalistic thinking, as is the special creation of humans by God. But naturalism is not the only pair of glasses on the market.

NOTES

1. See, for example, Job 38–39 and Psalm 104.

2. This is not to be thought of as a form of semi-deism. Semi-deism would teach that God did a series of creative acts but was not involved in the subsequent maintenance of the universe.

3. See chapter 5, under "God Is the Eternal Creator" and "God Has a Goal in Creation."

4. This assertion is plainly false. What the making of life in a test tube by a scientist would show is that mind acting on matter could produce life – which is precisely what Christians claim that God actually did.

5. Paul Davies, "E.T. and God," *Atlantic*, September 2003, www.theatlantic.com/magazine/archive/2003/09/et-and-god/376856.

6. Theistic evolution is sometimes called "evolutionary creationism" (Denis Alexander), "biologos" (Francis Collins), or "evotheism."

7. We should also note that, in any case, it would be rash to equate the word translated "kind" in Genesis 1 with our modern term *species*. The term *type* might be more appropriate as a translation.

8. Rabbi Jonathan Sacks, *The Great Partnership: Science, Religion, and the Search for Meaning* (2011; repr., New York: Schocken, 2012), 363.

9. Sacks, *Great Partnership*, 365, italics in original.

10. Francis Collins, *The Language of God: A Scientist Presents Evidence for Belief* (New York: Free Press, 2006), 205.

11. Pope John Paul II, "Message to the Pontifical Academy of Sciences on Evolution," 22 October 1996.

12. Collins, *Language of God*, 199.

13. Collins, *Language of God*, 200–201.

14. This view seems also to have been that of C. S. Lewis, although his scepticism about the adequacy of the evolutionary account appears to have grown over the years; see "Is Theology Poetry?" in *They Asked for a Paper: Papers and Addresses* (London:

Geoffrey Bles, 1962), 150–65; see also Gary B. Ferngren and Ronald L. Numbers, "C. S. Lewis on Creation and Evolution: The Acworth Letters, 1944–1960," *PSCF* 48 (March 1996): 28–33, www.asa3.org/ASA/PSCF/1996/PSCF3-96Ferngren.html.

15. We note that this looks very much like a special "intervention" by God.

16. Behe is at pains not to identify the designer in order not to confuse the science with the theology.

17. Simon Conway Morris, *Life's Solution: Inevitable Humans in a Lonely Universe* (Cambridge: Cambridge University Press, 2003), 330.

18. Needed for the production of the necessary heavy elements.

19. The word *evolution* in the phrase "theistic evolution" tends to cover more than biological evolution. The prebiotic phase has, however, nothing to do with evolution in the sense of (neo-)Darwinism, which, of course, presupposes by definition that life already exists.

20. This common objection is essentially that of David Hume, and I address it both in my *Cosmic Chemistry: Do God and Science Mix?* (Oxford: Lion Hudson, 2021), chapter 6, and in the last two chapters of my *Gunning for God: Why the New Atheists Are Missing the Target* (Oxford: Lion Hudson, 2011).

21. Denis Alexander, *Creation or Evolution: Do We Have to Choose?* (Oxford: Monarch, 2008), 38–39, emphasis added.

22. Alexander, *Creation or Evolution*, 31.

23. See C. S. Lewis, *Miracles* (1947; repr., New York: Macmillan, 1978), 55–62; see also my detailed discussion of this in *Gunning for God*, 165–86.

24. Although we should not forget that Jesus' resurrection was predicted.

25. For an excellent account of God's relationship to creation, see C. John Collins, *The God of Miracles: An Exegetical Examination of God's Action in the World* (Wheaton, IL: Crossway, 2000).

26. Of course, if science is *defined* as the study of reproducible regularities, then the assertion is tautologous. But the whole history of the universe is not reproducible, so that science, thus defined, could have nothing to say about it!

27. For a comprehensive contemporary exposition of the Augustinian view in relation to modern science, see Alister McGrath's Gifford Lectures, published as *A Fine-Tuned Universe: The Quest for God in Science and Theology* (Louisville, KY: Westminster John Knox, 2009).

28. See Lennox, *Cosmic Chemistry*, chapter 6.

29. That is one of the reasons I think I am, in principle, no more a "God of the gaps" man than C. S. Lewis was or Francis Collins is when they assign the gulf between animals and human beings to God's special conferment of his image.

30. We might just note that the heavens come before the earth. Cosmology says the same, of course.

31. See Hugh Ross, *The Genesis Question: Scientific Advances and the Accuracy of Genesis*, 2nd ed. (Colorado Springs: NavPress, 2001), 21.

32. In connection with the idea of perspective from a time rather than a spatial point of view, it has been suggested that we need to factor in Einstein's famous discovery that time is relative when attempting to understand the nature of the days of Genesis 1; see Gerald L. Schroeder, *Genesis and the Big Bang: The Discovery of Harmony between Modern Science and the Bible* (New York: Bantam, 1990).

33. See Lennox, *Cosmic Chemistry*, chapter 9.

34. No detail is given of what precise processes are subsumed under the statement "Let the earth bring forth" (Genesis 1:24). The crucial thing is that it did not happen without the direct activity of the word of God. This is another instance of "all things were made through him" (John 1:3).

35. See Richard Dawkins, *The Blind Watchmaker: Why the Evidence of Evolution Reveals a Universe without Design*, rev. ed. (1986; repr., New York: Norton, 1996), 5.

36. Quoted in Gerhard Schramm, "Synthesis of Nucleosides and Polynucleotides with Metaphosphate Esters," in *The Origins of Prebiological Systems and of Their Molecular Matrices*, ed. S. W. Fox (New York: Academic Press, 1965), 310, discussion section.

37. Richard Dawkins, *The Greatest Show on Earth: The Evidence for Evolution* (London: Free Press, 2009), 421.

38. I have considered these recent developments in much more detail in *Cosmic Chemistry*, chapter 19.

39. Bill Gates, *The Road Ahead*, rev. ed. (New York: Penguin, 1996), 228.

40. Amir D. Aczel, *Probability 1: The Book That Proves There Is Life in Outer Space* (New York: Harvest, 1998), 88.

41. For this general point, see my *Cosmic Chemistry*, chapter 11.

42. Leon Brillouin, *Science and Information Theory*, 2nd ed. (New York: Academic Press, 1962), 269.

43. Paul Davies, *The Fifth Miracle: The Search for the Origin and Meaning of Life* (New York: Simon & Schuster, 1999), 120, italics in original. "Specific randomness" is a technical concept used in connection with information.

44. For more detail on this central issue, see my *Cosmic Chemistry*, chapter 10, and also Stephen Meyer, *Signature in the Cell: DNA and the Evidence for Intelligent Design* (San Francisco: HarperOne, 2009).

45. Alexander, *Creation or Evolution*, 333.

46. Davies, "E.T. and God."

47. See Lennox, *Cosmic Chemistry*, part 4.

48. Steve Jones, *The Language of Genes: Solving the Mysteries of Our Genetic Past, Present and Future* (1993; repr., New York: Anchor, 1995), 41–42; see also Lennox, *Cosmic Chemistry*, chapter 9, for some amplification of this point.

49. Denis Noble, *The Music of Life: Biology beyond Genes* (Oxford: Oxford University Press, 2006), 130.

50. Noble, *Music of Life*, 31–32.

51. Jerry Fodor and Massimo Piattelli-Palmarini, "Survival of the Fittest Theory: Darwinism's Limits," *New Scientist*, 3 February 2010, 28–31, https://massimo.sbs.arizona.edu/sites/massimo.sbs.arizona.edu/files/publications/JF_MPP_darwinisms_limits.pdf. A fuller account is given in their book *What Darwin Got Wrong* (London: Profile, 2010).

52. Jerry Fodor, "Why Pigs Don't Have Wings," *London Review of Books* 29, no. 20 (18 October 2007), www.lrb.co.uk/the-paper/v29/n20/jerry-fodor/why-pigs-don-t-have-wings, emphasis added.

53. William B. Provine, *The Origins of Theoretical Population Genetics*, rev. ed. (1971; repr., Chicago: University of Chicago Press, 2001), 199–200.

54. Robert G. B. Reid, *Biological Emergences: Evolution by Natural Experiment* (Cambridge, MA: MIT Press, 2007).

55. Christopher S. Rose, review of *Biological Emergences: Evolution by Natural Experiment* by Robert G. B. Reid, in *Integrative and Comparative Biology* 48, no. 6 (December 2008): 871–73, https://academic.oup.com/icb/article/48/6/871/839346.

56. Reid, *Biological Emergences*, 2.

57. See Lennox, *Cosmic Chemistry*, chapter 5, in "Reductionism" section.

58. Rose, review of *Biological Emergences*, 871–73.

59. See Lennox, *Cosmic Chemistry*, chapter 19.

60. Robert Laughlin, *A Different Universe: Reinventing Physics from the Bottom Down* (New York: Basic Books, 2005), 168–69.

GENERAL INDEX